Poetry is 'an exciting island, with
with people. Maybe it's a slightly
times magical or ridiculous — poe

Adrian Mitchell, introduction, *Th*

The intention of *Universal Verse* is to celebrate and to promote an interest in contemporary and classic poetry for children. We hope that it will provide a whole range of suggested poetry titles that will enthral children of all ages.

Universal Verse

Poetry for Children

| *A guide edited by* | DEBORAH HALLFORD & EDGARDO ZAGHINI |

Contributors   MICHAEL ROSEN
MORAG STYLES
JOHN FOSTER
MANDY COE
GABY MORGAN
JANE RAY
JANETTA OTTER-BARRY

BARN OWL BOOKS

FIRST PUBLISHED IN 2006 BY BARN OWL BOOKS,
157 FORTIS GREEN ROAD, LONDON N10 3LX
BARN OWL BOOKS ARE DISTRIBUTED BY FRANCES LINCOLN
4 TORRIANO MEWS, TORRIANO AVENUE, LONDON NW5 2RZ
TEXT COPYRIGHT © 2006 BARN OWL BOOKS
FOREWORD COPYRIGHT © 2006 MICHAEL ROSEN
THE OPINIONS, SELECTIONS AND REVIEWS IN THIS BOOK
ARE NOT NECESSARILY THOSE OF BARN OWL BOOKS
ALL RIGHTS RESERVED

ISBN 0 903105 61 8
ISBN 13-978-1-903015-61-2

COVER DRAWING AND ILLUSTRATIONS BY JANE RAY
BOOK DESIGN BY DOUGLAS MARTIN
SET IN MONOTYPE SPECTRUM
PRINTED AND BOUND IN CHINA FOR IMAGO

THIS BOOK IS FUNDED BY ARTS COUNCIL ENGLAND

A special thankyou to everyone who contributed to this publication: Rachel Anscombe, Bridget Carrington, Mandy Coe, Jemma Cook, John Foster, Ferelith Hordon, Shelley Jacobsen, Rebecca Jones, Ann Jungman, Douglas Martin, Gaby Morgan, Paula O'Connor, Janetta Otter-Barry, Erif Petch, Jane Ray, Michael Rosen, Jacqueline Saphra, Anna Small, Nicola Smyth, Mandy Southern, Elizabeth Strick, Morag Styles, Miriam Valencia, and also to the many people who have given support and advice: Terence Ellis, Chris Holifield, Nicky Potter, Sally Robins, Siân Williams, Frances Lincoln and all the publishers who have submitted books for inclusion in this guide.

This publication could not have come about without the support of Arts Council England, Barn Owl Books and the Children's Bookshow.

Arts Council England supports a range of literature projects through their funding scheme, Grants for the Arts, and through their portfolio of regularly funded organisations. They recognise the transforming power of the arts in relation to young people.

Barn Owl Books is a small publishing house that specialises in publishing out-of-print children's books. They publish about eight books a year and their list includes Jacqueline Wilson, Michael Rosen, Malorie Blackman, Quentin Blake and a whole host of other authors. Barn Owl is delighted to branch out and be the publisher of *Universal Verse*, which is a terrific project and exciting to participate in.

The Children's Bookshow was set up in 2003 by Siân Williams and is supported by Arts Council England. It is a national tour of children's writers and illustrators who perform in theatres throughout England during October and November of each year. A programme of school workshops runs alongside the tour. Each tour has a theme; these have included Poetry, Folk and Fairy Tales and Translation.

P oetry is 'an exciting island, with valleys full of animals and palaces packed with people. Maybe it's a slightly foreign island, sometimes dangerous, sometimes magical or ridiculous – poetry is a wild island well worth exploring'.

Adrian Mitchell, introduction, *The Orchard Book of Poems*, Orchard Books, 1996

The intention of *Universal Verse* is to celebrate and to promote an interest in contemporary and classic poetry for children. We hope that it will provide a whole range of suggested poetry titles that will enthral children of all ages.

Included in the guide are over 200 books that are currently in print in the UK, reviewed by a team of independent experts, together with articles written on topics that will help to stimulate debate about poetry and a useful information section. Michael Rosen's foreword considers how 'poetry needs to be free to be explored'; Morag Styles examines the historical perspective of British poetry for children; John Foster writes on the complexities of compiling poetry anthologies; Mandy Coe discusses the teaching of poetry in schools and gives some practical advice, while Gaby Morgan and Janetta Otter-Ray give two different publishing perspectives.

Every effort has been made to select as eclectic a mix as possible of individual poetry collections and anthologies including both classic and contemporary verse. However, we were disappointed to discover that so many well-loved titles are now out of print. Although there seem to have been fewer poetry titles published during the last year and a perception that there are more anthologies than individual poet collections, *Universal Verse* has managed to find an equal selection of both.

The tradition of poetry has been around since time began – long before writing was invented – and the oral tradition of handing down rhymes and stories continued through the generations. Today, many people live without poetry and lose out on the chance to experience the vast array of wonderful poets both past and present. Poetry is a marvellous way of promoting the use and beauty of language and children need to be able to explore and enjoy poetry in all its different guises. Reading a poem aloud, written by any of the outstanding poets featured in this publication, will encourage children to explore language and humour, and even begin to write their own poetry.

How to use the guide

Universal Verse has been divided into four age categories: under 5, 6-8, 9-11 and 12+. Within each age category the books are split into individual poetry collections and anthologies. The books are then listed in alphabetical order of title within each section. The age categories are intended to act only as a broad guideline; in fact, many of the books will appeal to a wider age-range, including adults.

In partnership with Barn Owl Books, the Children's Bookshow and the Poetry Book Society, and supported by Arts Council England, we have been able to produce a guide that we hope will prove to be a useful resource.

Deborah Hallford and Edgardo Zaghini (Editors)

People must have been making up poems for children ever since there have been children. How else do you get them through teething, mumps and grazes? But then children must have been making up poems for as long as they've noticed each other. How else do they decide who's the next person to play, what rhythm you skip to or clap hands to? So the poems that children read, say, shout and sing have been around for a long time. It seems to me to be a great pity that this vast and wonderful tradition should have arrived at a point in the UK where it has become 'cabin'd, cribb'd, confin'd' by a set of instructions laid out in the anonymous documents on teachers' desks. If we think that arranging a meeting between children and poetry is a good idea, then it needs to be one that respects the rights of both parties. That's to say, poetry needs to be free to be explored and children need to be free to do the exploring. This means that we have to create poetry-friendly classrooms, corridors, playgrounds and schools. It means insinuating poetry into the spaces between things, letting it flow round the bricks and mortar.

I've often said, this might be nothing more than teachers writing out a poem on to a large piece of paper and pinning it up somewhere for a week or two. Nothing said, no explanation. No nit-picky little questions about adjectives or 'why is this so effective'? (Effective? Effective? Why can't I think it isn't effective? Why's it got to be 'effective', anyway? Can't it be slippery or happy or a bit like a tree?) And then maybe after a week or so, you could take that poem down and put up another one. And just see what happens . . . That's why poets write poems: to see what happens. It's not to have our adjectives counted, thank you very much.

Now that the country's children's and youth library services have been decimated and large areas of the country are without specialist children's book departments or shops, teachers can quite legitimately say that they haven't got time to seek out and find poems and poetry books for their classes. After all, they're too busy writing out the next day's learning objectives and yesterday's learning outcomes. (Question 1: what is the learning objective of this poem? Question 2: After it's been read, what was its outcome? Answer 1: The learning objective of this poem is that the children will have a good time reading and performing and talking about this poem. Answer 2: After it was read, I heard the children running about in the playground repeating the chorus. Inspector's report: This is rather an unsatisfactory analysis of the poetry lesson and makes no reference to the value of poetry for literacy, language development, citizenship training and number work.)

So, now we have an up-to-date guide to some of the best poetry out there along with some thoughtful words on what it's all about. Now all you need to do is get hold of a pile of these books, bring them into your classroom and sit about reading them. I've found that getting the children into groups of two or three and asking them to find ways of performing any poems that catch their eye will get them going. And remember:

Roses are red
Violets are blue
Most poems rhyme
This one doesn't

To write about the history of children's poetry in a short essay is quite a challenge and I must, therefore, confine myself to those who have made a major contribution to this genre, ignoring living poets and those, like Blake, whose work spans both adult and child audiences. What follows is a brief discussion of the works which made a difference to poetry for children from the early nineteenth to the late twentieth century. Until then, most poetry for children was didactic, although the sensational literature of the chapbooks (some of it in verse) provided light relief.

Romantic ideas began to percolate into children's poetry in Ann and Jane Taylor's *Original Poems for Infant Minds* (1804), followed by *Rhymes for the Nursery* in which appeared a matchless piece of nursery verse: "Twinkle, twinkle, little star. / How I wonder what you are! / Up above the world so high, / Like a diamond in the sky". This offered an invitation to young readers to dream and wonder, rather than be preached at, and there is no closure: "How I wonder what you are". The fact that the poem was parodied brilliantly by Lewis Carroll sixty years later demonstrates its significance in its own period: "Twinkle twinkle little bat. / How I wonder what you're at. / Up above the world so high, / Like a tea-tray in the sky".

The Star is so good that it is often ascribed to the oral tradition, but the Taylor sisters deserve to be recognised for the influential way they softened the genre, producing poetry that was deeply in tune with little children, sometimes employing loving, inconsequential language or 'motherese': "Come, dear, and sit upon my knee, / And give me kisses, one, two, three, / And tell me whether you love me, / My baby".

There is a direct line from the Taylor sisters to the greatest Victorian female poet, Christina Rossetti: "I'll nurse you on my knee, my knee, / My own little son; / I'll rock you, rock you, in my arms, / My least little one".

Rossetti employs an impressive range in *Sing-Song* (1872), her 'nursery rhyme book' — there are ditties, nonsense, riddles, colour and counting rhymes, as well as sad poems of grieving mothers and motherless babies. Other women poets from this period who deserve a mention from this period include Sara Coleridge whose 'Months of the Year' is still much anthologised ("January brings the snow. / Makes our feet and fingers glow."); Mary Howitt, a prolific writer whose *Sketches of Natural History* (1834) contained the famous "Will you come into my parlour, said the Spider to the Fly"; and Catherine Ann Dorset whose *The Peacock at Home* (1808) could be said to anticipate Lear's 'The Quangle Wangle's Hat': "Worms and frogs en friture for the web-footed fowl, / And a barbecued mouse was prepared for the Owl; / Nuts, grain, fruit and fish, to regale every palate, / And groundsel and chickweed served up in a sallad".

Nonsense verse has always been popular with children; it reached its height in the work of Edward Lear. Though he is best known for his development of the limerick, *A Book of Nonsense* (1871) contains his most inventive poetry. Like many humorists, Lear was a depressive and critics have traced the darkness in his poetry: "My life is a bore in this nasty pond / And I long to go out in the world beyond . . ."

But it is the originality and melodiousness of Lear's poetry (he was also a gifted musician and painter) that has lasted the test of time. 'The Owl and the Pussycat' was voted the Nation's favourite children's poem in 2000. Writing about adult responses to it in *Signal*, the poet John Mole insightfully describes it as: "exquisitely heartbreaking, not because reading it becomes some sort of sentimental reminder of a lost childhood, but because its simplicity so perfectly embodies the realities of life. We have learned the consequences of tarrying too long . . . and yet the power of the poem's closing lines . . . holds innocence and experience in an image which is simultaneously welcoming and valedictory". (Mole 2001)

Other poetic humorists worth noting are, of course, Carroll (best, I think, in the songs that punctuate the two Alice books, such as 'Jabberwocky' and 'The Walrus and the Carpenter'), Hilaire Belloc who brought his deliciously over-the-top cautionary verse to a wider audience (such as *The Bad Child's Book of Beasts*, 1896), and the earlier, lesser known, Thomas Hood: "Ben Battle was a soldier bold / And used to war's alarms; / But a cannon-ball took off his legs, / So he laid down his arms".

It was a Scot who changed children's poetry forever. Robert Louis Stevenson's *A Child's Garden of Verses* (1885) has never been out of print, perhaps because he was the first poet for the young to write both as if in the voice of a child and in the first person: "At evening when the lamp is lit, / Around the fire my parents sit; / They sit at home and talk and sing, / And do not play at anything". E. V. Lucas, a literary critic and Stevenson's contemporary wrote of *A Child's Garden*: "It stands alone. There is nothing like it, so intimate, so simply truthful, in our language, in any language . . . he has recaptured in maturity the thoughts, ambitions, purposes, hopes, fears, philosophy of the child".

Of course, Stevenson uses considerable adult artistry to appear childlike in the poetry, but the quality of the writing and his treatment of play, as well as his exploration of how adulthood inevitably involves the loss of childhood, are some of the reasons for its longevity: "For, long ago, the truth to say, / He has grown up and gone away, / And it is but a child of air / That lingers in the garden there".

Walter de la Mare is the key poet of the first half of the twentieth century: "Slowly, silently, now the moon / Walks the night in her silver shoon; / This way and that, she peers and sees / Silver fruit upon silver trees . . .". The creed by which he lived and wrote was based on the premise that childhood holds the key to life and that age brought stupidity, not greater wisdom. He was a great observer and technician, crafting his poems with lyric skill, great attention to detail and the gift of storytelling. He was also an important anthologist.

Eleanor Farjeon and A. A. Milne are also significant poets of this period. Farjeon's 'Morning Has Broken' is versatile enough to be a popular hymn still sung in primary schools today, as well as a famous rock lyric. *The Children's Bells* (1957) contains her personal selection gleaned from the many books of verse she wrote during a long life, while some of her lesser-known poems have been collected by Anne Harvey in *Something I Remember* (1987). Milne's *When We Were Very Young* (1924) and *Now We Are Six* (1927) had huge sales and mostly rave reviews when they were published and still delight many children today. If Milne's depiction of childhood can seem a little dated and privileged, it's worth remembering that he was also an excellent craftsman of light verse who could sometimes look at the world from a child's point of view almost as convincingly as Stevenson. He created unforgettable characters like the dreadfully bossy James James Morrison Morrison Wetherby George Dupree; or Bad Sir Brian Botany who "had a battleaxe with great big knobs on; / He went among the villagers and blipped them on the head"; or the "two little bears who lived in the wood / And one of them was bad and the other was good"; or Mary Jane who loathed rice pudding, or Emmeline whose hands were "purfickly clean". Milne was a master within a limited canvas.

Before the sweeping changes that were about to take place in children's poetry in the 1970s, two very significant poets produced their first collections for the young: Ted Hughes *Meet My Folks* (1961), and Charles Causley *Figgie Hobbin* (1970). Both were equally well known for their adult writing; both continued to publish outstanding poetry for children throughout their lives. Causley was a subtle balladeer whose work contains the ring of the storyteller, a feel for musical language, often a hint of something mysterious or even sinister that is left unexplained. It is rooted in folklore, often deriving from his native Cornwall, and steeped in the oral tradition and the ancient magic of words. He was also one of the finest anthologists of his age.

Ted Hughes was Poet Laureate and widely considered to be the most distinguished British poet of his generation. His speciality was a profoundly realistic yet numinous nature poetry which Hughes delivered with 'affection': "One can communicate with children in a simple and whole way – not because they're innocent, but because they're not yet defensive ... providing one moves with affection".

Despite the relentless realism, much of Hughes' poetry is set in a mystical landscape and at times his tone can be as visionary as Blake's. *Collected Animal Poems: What is the Truth?* (1984) is his masterpiece, but titles like *Collected Animal Poems: The Iron Wolf* (1995) and *The Mermaid's Purse* (1999) are also accessible for young readers. If his work is too strong for some tastes, particularly those who prefer to apply rose tinted spectacles to childhood, he offers poetry of power and potency to readers who can rise to the challenge.

Children have been well served by so many poets of the past. It is to be hoped that publishers will keep some of those key collections in print so that this wonderfully varied poetry is still available to young readers of the future.

This essay drew on my chapter on Poetry in Peter Hunt's *Routledge International Encyclopedia of Children's Literature* (2006).

Compiling a poetry anthology can be compared to doing a jigsaw puzzle. However, whereas at the start of doing a jigsaw puzzle you have the complete picture already before you, in the case of a poetry anthology you often only have a general idea of what the book will contain.

Exactly how many pieces of the jigsaw you have at the beginning will depend on the type of anthology and the proportion of new poems you plan to include. If it's a general anthology on the subject of school, for example, you may be planning to include a mixture of classic poems, contemporary favourites and specially written poems. In that case, you will have a clear idea of some of the contents at an early stage. If, on the other hand, you are compiling a book of mainly new poems about how to survive school or how to embarrass your teacher, you may initially have only a handful of poems.

Similarly, you may have a clear idea of the structure of the book at an early stage or you may only discover the best structure during the compilation process. If it is a book of animal poems, you may opt to arrange the poems alphabetically according to the animals' names or to put the poems into sections, according to the types of animals – pets, wild animals, zoo animals etc. Alternatively, if you are compiling a humorous book of completely crazy poems, the majority of which are to be new, previously unpublished poems, then you may wait to see what comes in before deciding on a structure.

The clearer idea you have of the structure, the easier it is to draft the letter inviting poets to submit poems for consideration. A major change in the nature of anthologies over the past thirty years is that most of them now contain a considerable number of new poems. In the past, anthologists tended to rely on finding the poems they required by trawling through previously published anthologies and single-author collections. This often led to a similarity between anthologies with the same poems appearing time and again.

Nowadays, anthologists are in contact with many established and aspiring children's poets who are willing either to write new poems or to draw the anthologist's attention to previously published poems which might be suitable for inclusion. Today, the main task when compiling an anthology is to sift through the mass of material you receive in response to a request for poems.

This is both frustrating and rewarding. The reason it is frustrating is because so many of the poems are clearly not what you are looking for. Many of them, from aspiring poets, fail to pass the first test – do they immediately grab your attention? If they don't, they are hardly likely to grab children's attention! Others, although they might have an unusual twist to them, are rejected because they are simply not well enough crafted. Or it may be a good poem, but not suitable for that particular anthology.

So what are you looking for? Above all, you are looking for something that the reader will respond to either, if it is a humorous poem, because it will make them laugh or, if it is a serious poem, because it will make them reflect on the experience that is described or see the world differently. Secondly, the poem needs to be written in language that is accessible to the child reader. Thirdly, it needs to "stand out in a crowd", perhaps because it encapsulates an experience, describes something by drawing an unusual comparison or is humorous in a quirky way. When you are sifting through the pile of submissions and you come across a poem that you know instinctively is right, that is what makes it rewarding.

Once you have made your initial choice, you have to look at the selection as a whole. If it is a general anthology you need to ensure there is a balance between the light-hearted and the serious. The chances are there are some gaps. That is when you turn to your bookshelf and trawl through your library of poetry books to find previously published poems to fill them. Whether you choose in-copyright or out-of-copyright material will depend on the permissions budget that you have agreed as part of your contract. Unfortunately financial constraints sometimes mean that you do not necessarily plug the gaps with what you consider to be the most suitable poems, but instead you use ones that incur no permissions charges.

The final task is to put the selected poems into an order. Whether or not the book is to be divided into sections, the positioning of each poem is important. Readers tend to dip into poetry books, so, as one of my editors once put it, you need to arrange the selection so that a poetry book can be read backwards as well as forwards. The juxtaposition of poems is important too: you do not want to place a poem on great-gran having dementia next to one about Uncle Albert's false teeth falling out. You also need to find a poem to start with that will set the right tone for the book and one to end with that will bring the book to a conclusion.

So the first draft of the jigsaw is completed and ready for submission to the publisher, together with 'the best of the rest' – a number of additional poems that can be substituted for any in your selection that your editor feels are not quite right for some reason. Almost invariably following a meeting with the editor the jigsaw is reshaped in some way. Perhaps the sections are reordered to give the book a snappier start or a number of substitutions are made.

Once the selection is finalised, it is time to discuss finding an appropriate illustrator or illustrators. Sometimes the book is compiled with a particular illustrator in mind. Over the years I have collaborated with Korky Paul on a series of collections, but more often than not, an illustrator with a suitable style has to be found after the compilation is completed.

In due course, the illustrations are drawn and the book is published. In recent years, the main market for anthologies has been schools. The National Literacy Strategy includes poetry as an integral part of the curriculum and, as more and more schools run book weeks and invite writers into schools, there are a number of poets, myself included, who regularly visit schools to give performances and run workshops.

The value of such visits is enormous. The performances are basically entertainment designed to stimulate an interest in and enthusiasm for poetry by making it fun. But the inclusion of a number of poems on issues such as bullying, homelessness and poverty can demonstrate the power of poetry to deal with serious subjects. Most performers also include a question-and-answer session during which the writer can provide insights into the writing process. The workshops provide an opportunity for the children to play with words and to be creative, to experiment in their writing and to draft and redraft it, free from the constraints of formulaic time-limited tasks designed to improve their test scores.

Mandy Coe

W hy poetry in schools? As a poet I am biased. Writing is a pleasure for me. But just as pleasurable is the 'state of being' that enables me to write. After all, to write about things we must notice them first. When children are writing poetry they become curious and observant (a wonderful state of being for young people). Their eyes open wider, they sit up. You know that look … *they are interested.* They take up their pen and paper and go away inside themselves to formulate thoughts, curving their hand around the paper as if the words might fly away. In my experience of working in schools, the common-est feedback is: *We learned to use our imagination.*

T. S. Eliot said: "Genuine poetry can communicate before it is understood," and although we study styles, count syllables and discover techniques, poetry is *about* whatever the *poem* is about. That everyone's response is subjective is one of the reasons why poetry appeals to children. Even in the earliest years a child will be drawn to a particular poem over and over again without having to know why. Whatever our culture or language, narrative poetry, counting games, nonsense rhymes, all seem to embody the mother tongue.

It is well known that reading and writing poetry has a positive impact on literacy and confidence levels, and these additional benefits are hugely enhanced when the adult teaching it values poetry as an artform in itself. Indeed, when poetry is delivered solely for its 'side-effects' its power can be horribly reversed. Many of us can recall a time when poetry was meted out to us like a brimming spoonful of cod-liver oil – the poem being presented as a diagnostic tool to analyse verse structure or test understanding of subject matter. Years later, adults who went through this still shudder at the very thought of poetry.

If it is enjoyment that keeps a child plugged in to literacy – the thrill, the laugh, the puzzlement – then poetry comes up trumps. With their rhythms, imagery, narrative and mystery, poems are short, re-readable and – with children taking turns to read and listen – democratic. It is often the quiet child who shines, or the student struggling with language who comes up with the startling metaphor. I would argue that poetry is one of the most child-centred, literacy-friendly artforms we have available in schools.

Why bring poets into schools? Many authors trace their ambition back to encouragement received from a teacher or writer. When he was the Children's Laureate, Michael Morpurgo stated that a writer visiting a school could help a child "become a reader for life, and maybe a writer too." He is not alone in believing this. The UK has a long tradition of teachers, writers or project co-ordinators developing exciting projects involving writers and schools.

A visit from a poet creates a number of unique opportunities: a chance for pupils and staff to work alongside a published writer; a focus for an arts event (resulting in a performance, a display or an anthology); or, through INSET, bringing new methods and ideas to the classroom. A visiting poet can work with your pupils in the classroom, an art gallery or even, as with the schools writing in response to the Antony Gormley statues in Crosby, on a beach!

A Poet's visit can celebrate a special event such as Book Week or National Poetry Day. It can be a one-day visit or take place over a longer period through a residency. It is worth doing a bit of investigation as to what length of visit and which poet will be best for you. The Poetry Society, the National Association of Writers in Education, Writing Together, Apples and Snakes, Live Literature Scotland, the Arts Council are but a few national organisations who regularly work with poets in schools. All of these organisations will give you advice on how to find a writer or will work in partnership with you to deliver a project.

What funding is available? There are many options, and joint funding is one of them. Consider the benefits of developing a writers-in-schools project alongside a local arts organisation, your public library, or other schools. Poets often enjoy working across the curriculum, so in secondary schools the bill does not always have to end up with the English Department. For comprehensive information about funding for schools go to *www.readingconnects.org.uk* and click on Funding.

Poetry-friendly schools: never send a letter out without a student's poem on it! With computers it is incredibly simple to reduce text and fit it somewhere on the page. Make illustrated poetry-posters, or poetry-bookmarks for the public library. Encourage teachers and students to read a poem aloud at assemblies or PTA meetings.

Build up a stock of good poetry books for the classroom and the library. Join the Children's Poetry Bookshelf *www.childrens poetrybookshelf.co.uk* and you will be sent a selection of the best children's poetry books published along with worksheets to encourage the children to write their own poems in response to each book. On its website, the CPB also has a recommended list of poetry books for schools. Encourage readers' and writers' groups in school; they can review books, compile anthologies of students' work and co-ordinate sections of a writer's visit, for example the question and answer session.

If your teachers are unsure about poetry, book a writer to deliver an INSET session (*Poetryclass* was designed with this in mind) or have a look at the residential courses offered by the Arvon Foundation for teachers or children *www.arvonfoundation.org*

Poetry-friendly classrooms: take a look at the wonderful world of poetry resources for teachers. Try the Poetry Society's *Poetryclass www.poetryclass.net*; or Barrington Stokes' website *www.barringtonstoke.co.uk*; or there's the BBC *www.bbc.co.uk/schools/ 411/literacy.shtml*; and the Poetry Zone *www.poetryzone.co.uk* . Let your class tune in to live literature through The Poetry Archive *www. poetryarchive.org* which has a site especially designed for teachers and an interactive children's archive where you can hear the poets being interviewed and reading their work.

Poetry is a great way for children to find their voice, and if you want to develop regular creative writing workshops in the classroom a good place to start is with the book *Jumpstart: The Poetry Book for Secondary Schools* (The Poetry Society). Edited by Cliff Yates, this book is full of insight and ideas as to how to encourage the reading and writing of poetry in secondary schools. For primary years, *The Poetry Book for Primary Schools* (The Poetry Society) edited by Anthony Wilson and Siân Hughes provides a wonderful selection of poems, interviews, games and lesson ideas.

Compile a class anthology of favourite poems written by students or published authors. Illustrate them. Display a 'poem of the week'. Teachers can model the importance of poetry in everyday life by sharing a poem that has meant a lot to them. And above all, celebrate the mysteriousness of verse – it's okay if we don't 'get it' instantly. It is a poem's ability to unfold itself slowly through re-reading that makes poetry such a pleasure. As the writer Joseph Joubert said, "You will find poetry nowhere unless you bring some of it with you".

When I joined Macmillan Children's Books in 1993 they were just starting a new strand of poetry publishing – reasonably priced, cheerfully packaged poetry books full of poems that were immediate and fun. It was quite unusual at the time; poetry had spent far too many years being something difficult that most readers abandoned once they left school. We showed that poetry could be astonishingly popular, and children chose to buy our books with their own money! The first title in this new-look list was *Ere We Go*, a book of football poems compiled by David Orme. It sold fantastically well and has had constant praise for encouraging reluctant readers. In the past decade we have published over 200 poetry books, not bad for a list publishing into a niche market.

The list was a success and that helped us branch out to create a big poetry list – we were publishing 30 titles a year at one point – featuring a really wide range of poetry for children from 5 to 15. We publish hardback gift treasuries, collections from Charles Causley, Jenny Joseph and Valerie Bloom, and beautiful anthologies such as *Overheard on a Saltmarsh* by Carol Ann Duffy and *Sensational!* by Roger McGough. It gave us the opportunity to take risks on poets who were not known in the children's market, such as Stephen Knight, who wrote for us, and to create opportunities for poets to write themed collections such as *Fairy Poems* by Clare Bevan. In 1998 we published our first big book, *Read Me*, which remains our biggest-selling title. It was followed in 2000 with *The Works* by Paul Cookson, a book that can now be found in every school in the country. The backbone of the list has always been wonderful child-friendly, hugely popular anthologies about school, teachers, aliens, ghosts, love and so on from a whole family of poets including David Orme, Brian Moses, Paul Cookson, Pie Corbett, David Harmer and Nick Toczek.

The wonderful thing about running the Macmillan Children's Books poetry list is that it is the publishing home of an incredible community of poets. I speak to around ten poets on a weekly basis, but we have a database of over 250 poets that we write to when we are compiling anthologies and it is growing all the time. We work together to create the best books we can and I know that I can rely on them all to help me with poems and suggestions and to help each other, which shows amazing generosity of spirit in an increasingly commercial world. Most of the poets we publish work in schools, and we listen very carefully to the feedback they give us from teachers and children. Poets who work in schools are the most incredible publicity machines: they promote poetry, they promote themselves and they promote their publishers. It is worth taking them seriously.

I love poetry, I love the fact that you can match any mood with a poem, any season or emotion or event, and that you can look at a single page of verse and say, 'Yes, that is exactly it.' I am very lucky to have the opportunity to do something I really love and I hope that my passion and the passion of the poets I work with shines through in our publishing. Here's to the next 200 books.

At Frances Lincoln we strongly believe in the value of poetry and rhyme for all ages, from baby books right through to books for children at top primary level. Poetry is central to our publishing vision, and we see it as one of our most powerful ways to communicate with children.

As part of our growing list of poetry and rhyme books, we have produced several new titles in 2005 and 2006. A good rhyming text is a wonderful asset in a board book – it can be very short and yet great to read aloud to the youngest child – and Linzi West's *A Beach Ball Has Them All* and *Warm Sun, Soft Sand* are very short rhymes that help to build a sunny seaside atmosphere. And John Agard's *Wriggle Piggy Toes* (see review p 36) is an irreverent, warm-hearted collection of poems for babies and toddlers themed around a child's day.

For the nursery-age child action rhymes are a valuable way to develop cognitive and motor skills, and in *Hippety-hop Hippety-hay* (see review p 32) Opal Dunn has used a combination of traditional rhymes and her own verses, graded to match the child's development. For the slightly older child Opal has created a book of rhymes linked to games from around the world: *Acker Backa Boo!* (see review on p 37) is a book for playing with – and learning to read at the same time.

In picture story books a rhyming text can be the ideal way to tell a story and inspire an illustrator and Margaret Mahy's poetry is the perfect example of this. Her verse is so visually exciting, and makes that satisfying leap between real life and fantasy. Margaret Mahy is a master of pace and storytelling through verse, and her poems are full of wit and humour. In her latest book, *Down the Back of the Chair*, the verse and pictures by Polly Dunbar work seamlessly and explosively together. Reading this book aloud is a brilliant oral and visual experience for both storyteller and audience.

In a similar way Jackie Morris has been inspired by James Mayhew's poem *Can You See a Little Bear?* Here the rhyming couplets by James Mayhew introduce fantastic characters and first concepts in a gentle way, while asking the reader to find Little

Bear on every spread. The rhyme creates a springboard for the illustrator, who paints lavishly detailed scenes to pore over, beautifully balancing the simple verse.

Poetry is a wonderful way into non-fiction, too, and this is demonstrated in Benjamin Zephaniah's *We are Britain* (see review p 62). Benjamin linked up with the photographer Prodeepta Das, and came to us with an unusual proposal. He wanted to present personal portraits of 13 real British children in verse, accompanied by photographs, celebrating the children's cultural diversity as well as the universality of their lives. We were excited by this and felt that it would be a unique way of capturing a sense of 21st century Britishness as well as being completely in tune with the ethos of our multicultural publishing.

Even in novels and older fiction poetry has a part to play and *Hey Crazy Riddle* by Trish Cooke and *Butter-finger* by Bob Cattell and John Agard are exciting additions to our new multicultural fiction list. *Hey Crazy Riddle* is a collection of Caribbean tales awash with rhyme, wit and language play while *Butter-finger* combines calypsos with prose narrative in a way that really enriches the story.

And finally, we believe in the importance of poetry anthologies with a rich diversity of source and content. *Skip Across the Ocean* and *All the Colours of the Earth* (see reviews on p 41 and p 65) are two anthologies published by Frances Lincoln in the last few years. In *Skip Across the Ocean* Floella Benjamin collected rhymes from around the world, and for this book we felt it was important to print the poems in their original languages as well as English to give the flavour and look of the original verse. As Floella said in her introduction to the collection, "nursery rhymes are precious and should be shared by everyone. They are children's first introduction to rhythm, poetry and music, and pass on cultural values to the next generation." The selection includes poems from India, China, Africa and the Caribbean – great for the multicultural classroom.

We also wanted a stimulating collection for older children,

and the result is Wendy Cooling's *All the Colours of the Earth*. This multi-layered celebration of cultural diversity challenges children to think about the world – its richness as well as its inequalities.

Future poetry projects for 2007 and beyond range from an exuberant train-ride in verse for preschoolers – *Animals Aboard* by Andrew Fusek Peters and Jim Coplestone – to *Shapeshifters* by Adrian Mitchell and Alan Lee, an extraordinary, dramatic rendering of Ovid's *Metamorphoses*. So yes, we believe that poetry has the power to cross cultural boundaries, whether it's to demonstrate the richness of another culture or engage with universal themes. Either way, poetry is a vital and vibrant part of Frances Lincoln's publishing.

Bibliography

A Beach Ball Has Them All Linzi West (2005) £3.99 ISBN: I 84507 337 I

Warm Sun, Soft Sand Linzi West (2005) £3.99 ISBN: I 84507 342 8

Down the Back of the Chair Margaret Mahy, illustrated by Polly Dunbar (2006)
    HB £10.99 ISBN: I 84507 440 8

Can You See a Little Bear? James Mayhew, illustrated by Jackie Morris (2005)
    HB £10.99 ISBN: I 84507 298 7

Hey Crazy Riddle Trish Cooke, illustrated by Hannah Shaw (2006) PB £3.99
    ISBN: I 84507 378 9

Butter-finger Bob Cattell and John Agard, illustrated by Pam Smythe (2006)
    PB £4.99 ISBN: I 84507 376 2

Animals Aboad Andrew Fusek Peters and Jim Coplestone (2007)

Shapeshifters Adrian Mitchell and Alan Lee (2007)

"**P**oetry has always meant a lot to me. I think my appreciation of it came mainly from my mother. She sang and read to my sisters and me, and taught us nursery rhymes so that an enjoyment of words and rhythm was instilled in me from babyhood. She was an infant teacher all her working life and had a great interest, too, in the poetry of the playground. I went to a church school where hymns were sung every morning, and tho' the religion didn't stay with me, the power and majesty of some of those thundering hymns did. My father is a pianist and the soundtrack to my childhood was his practising. We sang with him too – folk songs and show songs, all with rich lyrics and fascinating, clever language.

As the parent of young children I came to appreciate that the books that stood reading again and again were the ones whose texts were nearer to poetry than prose, the ones that were lyrical, rhythmic and satisfying. As an illustrator I am aware of a need for rhythm in the line, composition and pace of a picture book.

I read poetry a lot – a newly discovered favourite being the Scottish poet Kathleen Jamie whose work I love".

The Orchard Book of Love Stories

Rapunzel, *Fairy Tales*, WALKER BOOKS

Beauty and the Beast, *Fairy Tales*, WALKER BOOKS

Romeo & Juliet, WALKER BOOKS

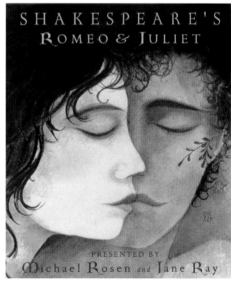

Romeo & Juliet, WALKER BOOKS

Jane Ray studied art and design at Middlesex University. Her main study was ceramics and she didn't start to illustrate until she left college. Her first published work was a series of greetings cards for Roger la Borde, followed by some book jackets, and eventually black-and-white illustrations for a poetry anthology with Orchard Books. Jane's first full-colour picture book was *A Balloon for Grandad* by Nigel Gray 1989, (Orchard Books). Since then she has illustrated numerous children's books, including *Fairy Tales* by Berlie Doherty, *Can You Catch a Mermaid?* (written and illustrated by Jane) and *The King of Capri* by Jeanette Winterson. She has recently finished working on a book for Bloomsbury called *The Lost Happy Endings* by Carol Ann Duffy, a wonderfully dark fairy tale which will be published next autumn, and is currently working on *Celtic Myths and Legends* for the Folio Society. *Little Prince Lugalbanda* will be published by Walker Books in May 2007, and Jane is about to start work on a story of her own for Orchard Books. Her work has exhibited regularly at Primavera, Cambridge and The Illustration Cupboard, London.

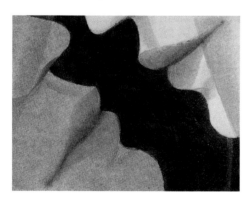

Romeo & Juliet, Walker Books

Alphabet Poem

Michael Rosen, illustrated by Hervé Tullet

MILET (2004) HB £10.99 ISBN: 1 84059 393 8

An original, thought-provoking and beautiful book for toddlers and young children and winner of the WOW! Award and the White Ravens Award in 2005. Rosen's words and Tullet's pictures combine to make a colourful, riotous and anarchic approach to the business of learning letters. The world turns on its head as shoes sing, computers cook cakes and monkeys make movies. This is a partnership between text and illustration in which neither would function without the other – Tullet has employed pen and ink, oils and acrylics, mono and a scorching colour palette to attempt to match the imaginative feats of Rosen's verse. How do you make ice-cream look itchy? Somehow, he manages it. The perfect antidote to 'A is for apple', though, with a typical sense of fun, that is exactly where this book begins. And yes, it ends at Zebra too, but the journey between is anything but predictable.

Hippety-hop, Hippety-hay

Opal Dunn, illustrated by Sally Anne Lambert

FRANCES LINCOLN (2001) PB £6.99 ISBN: 0 7112 1195 7

Hippety-hop, Hippety-hay contains a selection of interactive rhymes for nursery-age children. Opal Dunn is a specialist in early language development and the book is divided into three age categories: 2-12 months, 12-24 months and 24-36 months with each rhyme carefully selected for the appropriate age group. There is a combination of traditional and Dunn's own verse and individual section introductions provide useful information on child development. The rhymes are very short, ranging from four to eight lines, and cover a variety of subjects: animals, physical movements, weather, daily activities such as brushing your hair, dressing up and eating. There are suggestions for play activities to accompany the rhymes which are enhanced by Sally Ann Lambert's colourful illustrations. There is music for some rhymes at the back of the book as well as an index of first lines. This is an ideal book for parents to use with their babies or toddlers.

Moon Frog:
Animal Poems for Young Children

Richard Edwards, illustrated by Sarah Fox-Davies

WALKER BOOKS (2004) PB £5.99 ISBN: 1 84428 729 7

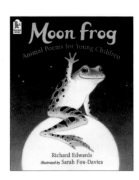

This highly original and entertaining collection of animal verse by Richard Edwards has poems about all kinds of animals, from the delightful 'Moon Frog' and 'Ozzie Octopus', who has the ideal anti-dote to being glum, to a spider who dances on a drum in 'Midnight' and the curious 'Banana Slugs'. The dentist mysteriously disappears in 'The Crocodile's Dentist' and beware of the hippopotomi when they open their mouths wide in 'Keep Well Back'. Many of the poems are nonsense verse but 'Open All the Cages' is a poignant poem about giving parrots their freedom. The animals get up to some strange antics too in 'The Café on the Corner' and 'The Worm Olympics'. The poems are accompanied by decorative illustrations by Sarah Fox-Davies.

Moon Zoo

Carol Ann Duffy, illustrated by Joel Stewart

MACMILLAN CHILDREN'S BOOKS (2004) PB £4.99 ISBN: 1 405 02050 4

Another other-worldly title from the team that produced the much-praised *Underwater Farmyard*, *Moon Zoo* is inhabited by baboons who flash their bottoms, an alien zookeeper with eight green arms and bouncing elephants. Duffy's approach to verse for children makes it no less sophisticated than her adult offerings – the elephants' trunks are "telescopes probing space / Pointing up at the Earth's blue face", while the moon itself is "a plate on the table of the sky, / Licked completely clean". Stewart's colourful illustrations float through the pages, the zoo's animals elegantly suspended in the weak moon gravity. This partnership cannot be bettered. A stimulating read that can be revisited again and again without ever becoming tiresome.

Nonsense ABC Rhymes

Richard Edwards, illustrated by Chris Fisher

OXFORD UNIVERSITY PRESS (2005) PB £5.99 ISBN: 0 19 911129 4

This book will help to make learning the alphabet fun. Each page has a letter with a rhyme and starts with a question: "What does 'A' stand for / Air, says the balloon", "What does 'B' stand for / Bristles, says the broom", and so on right through the alphabet. The rhymes are very memorable and featured towards the end of the book are further short 'ABC' rhymes – "Aa / A, A, Annie Bly / Ate an alligator pie" – to help reinforce the letters learnt in the earlier part of the text. Chris Fisher has provided exuberant illustrations to match the original nonsense rhymes from Richard Edwards, making this is an ideal book for reading or chanting aloud. Other titles in the series include *Nonsense Nursery Rhymes, Nonsense Counting Rhymes, Nonsense Animal Rhymes* and *Nonsense Christmas Rhymes*.

One, Two, Tree!

Anushka Ravishankar and Sirish Rao, illustrated by Durga Bai

TARA PUBLISHING (2003) HB £8.99 ISBN: 81 86211 80 2

A charming collaboration of rhyming text and richly coloured illustrations that creates an ideal way of learning to count. As a flock of birds abandon their tree, a steady posse of animals begin to climb it, from one dizzy ant, two dreamy lizards, three snoopy rats and so on, until the final ten hefty elephants! The ever-expanding tree happily accommodates them all, until finally there is room for no more and the birds decide to return. With a trick ending revealed on the last page, this absurd rhyming number book will delight children and adults alike. Durga Bai's bold dye-cut illustrations match the simple text perfectly. From the Gond tribe in central India, this is the artist's first children's book and there is an interesting profile on her at the back of the book.

The Quangle Wangle's Hat

Edward Lear, illustrated by Louise Voce

WALKER BOOKS (2006) PB £5.99 ISBN: 1 4063 0042 X

Edward Lear's famous story has been produced with new illustrations. It tells the simple story of the Quangle Wangle, who wears an extremely exciting and very large hat, but lives alone at the top of a tree and longs for visitors. This happy narrative goes on to describe all the animals that come to live on the Quangle Wangle's hat. The music of the language still works as well as it always did, and the subject matter lends itself perfectly to illustration. The simple, cheerful lines and bright colours are effective and evocative and the pictures full of movement. This is a timeless tale that will almost certainly delight any small child, offering the joys of Lear's wonderful rhyme that will provide a huge sense of enjoyment and of course a touch of madness to round it off.

Rhymes for Annie Rose

Shirley Hughes

RED FOX (1997) PB £6.99 ISBN: 0 09 946491 8

Rhymes for Annie Rose takes the focus away from Alfie, one of Shirley Hughes' best loved characters, into the world of his little sister, Annie Rose. With beautifully paced poems, action rhymes and lullabies the reader is given the eyes of a child, finding wonder and fun in everyday things. Along with her ever faithful big brother, Annie Rose sails the seas of her living room carpet, discovers the wonders of snow, builds castles and gets lost in a land of feet. Complementing each poem are beautiful watercolour and sketched illustrations; every picture adding to and expanding on the images created by the verse. This is a collection that, whether read cover to cover or dipped into, will evoke the child in every reader.

Riddledy Piggledy:
A Book of Rhymes and Riddles

Tony Mitton, illustrated by Paddy Mounter

DAVID FICKLING BOOKS (2004) PB £6.99 ISBN: 0 552 54819 7

A refreshing take on familiar themes, this volume starts out in traditional nursery rhyme territory and then, with the addition of intriguing riddles, moves the reader somewhere new. Each classic verse is preceded by one of Mitton's clue-ridden accompaniments, inviting you to guess what's coming next: "A cake marked B / that still feels hot. / Someone must be / missing it a lot"; turn the page to discover whether you were right or not in 'Pat-a-Cake, Pat-a-Cake'. The riddles themselves are often very funny and children (and adults) will get a lot of pleasure from puzzling out the answers, as well as from the nursery favourites themselves. They might even be inspired to compose their own. This is innovative and entertaining, and the colour illustrations complement Mitton's jokes and add to the sense of fun.

Tiger on a Tree

Anushka Ravishankar, illustrated by Pulak Biswas

TARA PUBLISHING (2002) HB £9.99 ISBN: 81 86211 35 7

A story about a wild tiger cub who wanders along the shores of a river and into a village looking for adventure. Suddenly, he is scared by a goat and looks for refuge in a tree. He is discovered by a group of vil-

lagers who are frightened and decide to capture him. They surround the tree and with the help of a net Tiger is trapped. Now they have to decide what to do with him! *Tiger on a Tree* is an internationally award-winning book written in Indian/English nonsense verse. The story has a charming simplicity with light verse spreading in waves through the pages. Full of rhythm and onomatopoeic words, this is a wonderful story to read aloud. Pulak Biswas' simplistic hand silk-screened illustrations complement the narrative with the use of the two colours, ("tigerish" black and orange, across white hand-made paper) and bring alive the expressive characters. (This review first appeared in *Outside In: Children's Books in Translation* published by Milet).

Wriggle and Roar!
Rhymes to Join in With

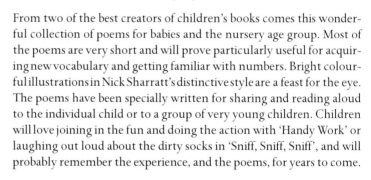

Julia Donaldson, Illustrated by Nick Sharratt

Macmillan Children's Books (2005) pb £4.99 isbn: 1 405 02166 7

From two of the best creators of children's books comes this wonderful collection of poems for babies and the nursery age group. Most of the poems are very short and will prove particularly useful for acquiring new vocabulary and getting familiar with numbers. Bright colourful illustrations in Nick Sharratt's distinctive style are a feast for the eye. The poems have been specially written for sharing and reading aloud to the individual child or to a group of very young children. Children will love joining in the fun and doing the action with 'Handy Work' or laughing out loud about the dirty socks in 'Sniff, Sniff, Sniff', and will probably remember the experience, and the poems, for years to come.

Wriggle Piggy Toes

John Agard, illustrated by Jenny Bent

Frances Lincoln (2005) hb £9.99 isbn: 1 84507 084 4

Follow the rhyme and rhythm in this book of very short verses especially for babies. Themed around a child's day from breakfast through to bedtime, these simple poems from internationally-acclaimed poet John Agard are written from a baby's perspective. A poem about being weighed provides a rhyme about a whale: "Wish I was a whale, / I'd tipple with my tail. / Wish I was a whale, / I'd topple that scale". The illustrations by Jenny Bent are close-up studies that make a baby's small world seem larger than life itself and complement the four-line verse on every page. This first book of poetry is suitable for any baby or toddler, and one that the whole family can share and read aloud.

Acker Backa BOO! Games to Say and Play from Around the World

Opal Dunn, illustrated by Susan Winter

FRANCES LINCOLN (2001) PB £5.99 ISBN: 0 7112 1662 2

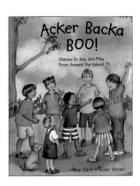

This is a worthy but slight book by a specialist in first and second language development. It includes games from all over the world. There are short sections on catch games, ball games, singing games and others. It gives the rhymes to use, an explanation of how to play the games and which country they are from. There are tips for parents and carers on how to get the best out of the games. Included are the words and explanations of some well-known UK games such as 'The Dusty Bluebells' and 'My father went to sea, sea, sea' as well as words and games that will be new to many. The idea of learning pre-reading language skills, attitudes and values through play and rhyme is not new. This book has a slightly old-fashioned feel both in content and through the muted coloured illustrations; nevertheless it would be a useful addition to a multicultural collection.

Animal Worlds

Illustrated by Paul Hess

ZERO TO TEN (2005) PB £6.99 ISBN: 1 84089 408 3

Big bold illustrations attract the attention as each page opens to reveal another animal from habitats ranging from the exotic to the familiar. Here the reader can meet well known types – the cow, the lion, the penguin and the bear, as well as more unusual specimens – the tapir, toucan and wildebeest. Each animal is accompanied by brief text in verse – verse selected to be short, humorous and catchy. It is perhaps a pity the publishers have not seen fit to acknowledge the source with each selection. These range from traditional rhymes to verses by Anne and Jane Taylor (18th century) and contemporary poets such as Jack Prelutsky. This is a quibble – as is the feeling that it would have been nice to have had a few more serious examples. A book to share, to read with relish and listen as the words are caught and repeated with gusto for their rhythm and rhyme.

Night-night, Knight and Other Poems

Chosen by Michael Rosen, illustrated by Sue Heap

WALKER BOOKS (1998) PB £2.99 ISBN: 0 7445 4884 5

This is a great introductory collection that includes a very useful preface, which gives hints and tips for reading poetry aloud with young children. A very good range of poems has been selected, from the old and familiar to the modern and contemporary. There are many different styles and tones for a child to get to grips with so they will certainly not be bored. Even if they are a bit too young for the text, the pictures will engage even the youngest children, as they are bright, simple and evocative. A great little collection, well chosen and produced.

The Orchard Book of Favourite Rhymes and Verse

Chosen by Margaret Mayo, illustrated by various artists

ORCHARD BOOKS (2001) PB £7.99 ISBN: 1 84362 305 6

A beautiful and colourful introduction to poetry for the home, school or library. This book comprises 40 poems accompanied by vibrant pictures by 22 illustrators. The poets range from Shakespeare, Lear and Walter de la Mare to contemporary favourites such as Giles Andreae and John Agard. There are classic nursery favourites such as 'The Wheels on the Bus' and 'Michael Finnigan', alongside less well-known poems that are sure to become future classics. The verses vary in length from a few lines to filling a double-page spread. This mixture of styles as well as the range of illustrations makes this the perfect book for dipping in and out of. It also means that children will not get bored if they read through the entire book in a single sitting. The quality of the layout, poems, illustrations and binding makes this anthology a timeless gem for readers, as well as listeners, whatever their age.

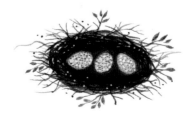

Poems for the Very Young

Selected by Michael Rosen, Illustrated by Bob Graham

KINGFISHER (2003) PB £8.99 ISBN: 0 7534 0022 7

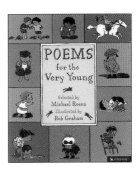

There is only one way to appreciate this anthology to the full: read it aloud, either to yourself or to a child or group of children. Doing so, you will hear the magical sounds of the words and the fluent musical rhythm that comes from each poem. As Michael Rosen says in his introduction "the core of this collection is a playful use of words and sounds". Here you will find traditional British poems as well as American, Australian, Philippine and Japanese. There are many short anonymous poems, but also many by very-well known poets like John Agard, John Foster, Eleanor Farjeon, Kit Wright, Jack Prelutsky and even a poem written by a ten-year-old child. Michelle Magorian's 'I Won't' is about an obstinate girl who will not wear a hat, while 'Hot Dogs Forever' by Sonia Dunn reflects upon the various ways in which a hot dog can be eaten, and there is also the delicious poem about 'Chocolate Milkshake' by Tania Mead. Kate Greenaway Medal winner Bob Graham's witty and funny illustrations are the perfect accompaniment to this superb anthology. This is a book that should be on the shelves of every school library.

Pudding and Pie: Favourite Nursery Rhymes

Chosen by Sarah Williams, illustrated by Ian Beck

OXFORD UNIVERSITY PRESS (2006)
PB £7.99 ISBN: 0 19 275477 7

Round and Round the Garden: Play Rhymes for Young Children

Chosen by Sarah Williams, illustrated by Ian Beck

OXFORD UNIVERSITY PRESS (2006)
PB £7.99 ISBN: 0 19 275478 5

Many of the best-loved rhymes are here in these two collections chosen by Sarah Williams. *Pudding and Pie* contains 40 nursery rhymes including some well-known favourites such as 'Little Jack Horner', 'Three Blind Mice' and 'Little Bo-Peep'. *Round and Round the Garden* contains over 30 traditional play rhymes including 'Incy Wincy Spider' and 'Pat-a-Cake'. Each play rhyme has clear step-by-step line drawings to follow the action on every page. Both books are clearly laid out with imaginative and striking illustrations by Ian Beck. The rhymes have been set to music on the accompanying CD, which is perfect for singalong, playtime and bedtime. These titles, along with further books in the series – *Oranges and Lemons* and *Ride a Cock Verse* – will provide a valuable collection of rhymes.

Ring o' Roses: Nursery Rhymes, Action Rhymes and Lullabies

Priscilla Lamont

FRANCES LINCOLN (1998) PB £5.99 ISBN: 0 7112 1245 7

When readers open this delectable picture book, they will be certain that Priscilla Lamont has chosen her all-time favourite poems to illustrate. Lamont's soft-focus pictures add a magical extra dimension to the well known and loved verses, and combine a traditional approach with carefully observed detail which links them to the twenty-first century child in general, and the reader in particular. 'To market, to market', for example, is headed by a picture which relates to the rhyme itself, while beneath Lamont shows a toddler being given a piggyback by her dad. Divided into sections as nursery rhymes, action rhymes and lullabies, every page is filled with lively, funny and perceptive pictures of babies, toddlers and small children sleeping, playing and learning about life. Words and music for the lullabies are included at the end of this delightful book.

Seaside Poems

Collected by Jill Bennett,
illustrated by Nick Sharratt
OXFORD UNIVERSITY PRESS (2006)
PB £7.99 ISBN: 0 19 275478 5

Tasty Poems

Collected by Jill Bennett.
illustrated by Nick Sharratt
OXFORD UNIVERSITY PRESS (2006)
PB £7.99 ISBN: 0 19 275478 5

Get ready to splash into the water at the seaside and taste oodles of noodles with these two collections of poems featuring some well-known contemporary poets including Judith Nicholls, Richard Edwards, Grace Nichols and John Agard. *Seaside Poems* are full of verse about what children like to do at the seaside – 'Let's do the flip-flop frolic', 'Imagining Mermaids' and Margaret Mahy's 'Goodness Gracious!' about a grandmother swimming out to sea! *Tasty Poems* shows that food can be fantastic fun with a wobbling jelly race and bouncing popcorn. There is also a delightful shape poem by Jack Prelutsky – 'Chocolate Milk', with the words winding round inside the straw from the milkshake to the little boy's mouth. Both collections are accompanied by colourful, humorous illustrations by award-winning artist, Nick Sharatt. These books are perfect for reading aloud.

Skip Across the Ocean: Nursery Rhymes from Around the World

Collected by Floella Benjamin, illustrated by Sheila Moxley
FRANCES LINCOLN (1998) PB £5.99 ISBN: 0 7112 1285 6

This anthology of nursery rhymes from six continents and 23 countries features some well-known verses such as 'Frère Jacques' and 'Ride a Cock Horse' and some which have never been written down before. Organised under four headings – lullabies, action rhymes, nature verse and a lucky dip – each poem is identified by its place of origin. Some are given in bilingual versions (where else would you find a Wampanoag lullaby?), some are given solely in their English translations. This is a diverse and unusual collection, featuring new rhymes, which will soon become favourites. Instructions for the action rhymes are included, so that you can get the most out of them. No other book will take you on a world journey as wide-ranging as this one, from Antigua to India, Uganda to Japan. Each choice is a winner, charming and unique. The rich colour illustrations help to keep the feel friendly and welcoming – essential when the content is largely unfamiliar.

Twinkle Twinkle Chocolate Bar

Compiled by John Foster, illustrated by various artists

OXFORD UNIVERSITY PRESS (1993) PB £8.99 ISBN: 0 19 276125 0

Another superb anthology compiled by John Foster for the very young that has a good selection of funny and descriptive rhymes and poems. They are loosely grouped together into themes which include food, nature and the seasons, animals, alphabet and number rhymes, playtime, bathtime, and going to bed. Two rhymes by Michael Rosen 'On the Beach' and 'Messing About' show what fun there is to be had at the seaside or just messing about. 'The Sandwich' by Tony Bradman covers a double-page spread, with an amazingly colourful illustration of a giant sandwich, which has become too big to eat. There is a nonsense rhyme by Trevor Millum, ' Valerie Malory & Sue Hu Nu' and a wonderful alphabet poem, 'An Alphabet of Horrible Habits' by Colin West. The longest poem in the book, spreading over four pages, is Dave Calder's 'This is the Key to the Castle', with brilliant illustrations by Korky Paul, about a big fat spider who lives in the cold dark cellar and weaves her web protectively around the key to the castle. Ideal for sharing and reading aloud.

A Bit of Nonsense

Edward Lear

SUMMERDALE (2005) HB £4.99 ISBN: 1 84024 457 7

Be prepared to immerse yourself in this delightful selection of classic nonsense poems by the outrageously funny Edward Lear. This is a small hardback edition containing Nonsense Songs, Nonsense Alphabet and Nonsense Limericks as well as the funny 'Foss the Cat' – a very short poem at the end of the book. In *A Bit of Nonsense* you will encounter the most incredible creatures and adventures: see how a Duck travels on the back of a Kangaroo or how the Table and the Chair go out for a walk or meet other imaginary creatures such as 'The Dong with the Luminous Nose'. Then there are the limericks: with the man with the long nose or the one with a beard and the screaming young lady of Russia. Edward Lear is well known for his absurd wit and this Christmas stocking-filler edition featuring classic illustrations by the author will be treasured by the child who reads Lear's poems for the first time or by an adult revisiting these old favourites.

A Children's Treasury of Milligan: Classic Stories and Poems

Spike Milligan

VIRGIN BOOKS (2001) PB £9.99 ISBN: 0 7535 0454 5

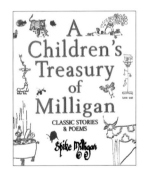

Spike Milligan (1918-2002) was one of the best and most-loved comed -ians as well as being an musician, poet, scriptwriter and novelist whose career spanned over 50 years. Divided into six sections under such zany headings as 'Silly Verse for Kids' – his first book written in 1959 – or 'Unspun Socks From A Chicken's Laundry', it is a compila-tion from his classic children's books with a list of contents at the beginning of each chapter. The poems are funny, clever, outrageous and witty. Each one is a superb creation and a sheer delight to read aloud and share. Most of the poems featured in this volume were written especially for Milligan's own children and grandchildren. How does an elephant "bend forward on all four knees" in 'The Elephant'? and what does 'Multikertwigo' mean? The title of this nonsense poem was a word that Spike's father used when he was a boy. Rude poems feature too: in 'Monkey', a cheeky animal shows his bum to a teacher! And there is even a poem dedicated to Prince

Charles, which is too unsavoury to mention. Included in this volume are also short stories like 'The Sad Happy Ending Story of The Bald Twit Lion', but predominantly the volume is made up of poems. The superb illustrations by the author himself and others have been specially commissioned for this gift edition. This is a treasury that you will want to keep on your bookshelf forever and revisit again and again, whether as a child or a grown-up.

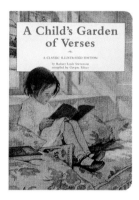

A Child's Garden of Verses

Robert Louis Stevenson

Compiled by Cooper Edens, illustrated by various artists

Chronicle Books (2004) board book £4.99 isbn: 0 8118 4168 5

This is a compilation of eight poems from the classic book *A Child's Garden of Verses*. The poems evoke the world and feelings of childhood. 'The Land of Counterpane', for instance, is about a child who lies sick in bed imagining a fantasy world where his own toys come alive and he becomes a giant overlooking the land. 'The Lamplighter' features a boy looking through his bedroom window and dreaming of becoming the lamplighter, who goes round the town at night lighting up the streets. In 'Foreign Lands' we encounter a child up a tree contemplating the whole world around him. These are all poems that focus on the essence of childhood and perfectly depict a child's imagination. Each verse is accompanied by a classic full-colour illustration. Artists featured include M. Didbin Spooner (1906), H. Willebeek Le Mair (1926), Jessie Willcox Smith (1905), Charles Robinson (1896) and others. This gives a taste of some of the best children's poems ever written and will hopefully encourage young readers to venture into the full edition containing all of Stevenson's verses. This is a concise but good compilation to share and read aloud again and again.

All the Best

Roger McGough, Illustrated by Lydia Monks

Puffin (2004) PB £7.99 ISBN: 0 141 31637 3

*Warning: this is not a poem. It's pretending to be a review!

Roger McGough's writing
Is certainly very exciting
With lots of poems about school
And others that are really cool.
My favourite is the *Head*
How I wish I wrote that instead!

Further along, we find another two
One about a *Snowman* and one about *Haiku*
Then another of a *Handfish*
And any subject you may wish.

The rhythm of each verse
Will make your tongue kick in reverse
They are ideal to read alone
But if in a group you want to tuck
Then go ahead and try your luck

Lydia Monks' illustrations
Are full of wacky inventions
They ideally match each verse
Which will make critics converse

I recommend this book to everyone
Even the Governor of San Juan
And for those who think poetry is in decay
Then try *All the Best* without delay!
Yes, try to read each poem alone, in classroom or assembly
Spread the word profusely
And the reward will be
That Mr McGough will thank you eter . . . nally

Ed Zaghini (2006)

Anything But a Grabooberry

Anushka Ravishankar, illustrated by Rathna Ramanathan

Tara Publishing (2002) HB £9.99 ISBN: 81 86211 43 8

A wacky book which aims to innovate by combining nonsense verse, by one of its pioneering Indian exponents, with bold typographical tricks by one of India's most radical book designers. Using two colours, red and green, the type forms shapes which suggest the words it is depicting. Sometimes the imagery is straightforward (the 'o' in 'orange' looks like the fruit); sometimes it needs to be thought about (the smudgy red typeface representing 'a black cloud'). The verse itself is exuberant and imaginative: "I want to be an elephant / or a packing trunk / or / maybe something smaller / like the big toe of a monk". The idea is to set off word associations, freeing the child's imagination from the bonds of logic, and the resulting book was the winner of a Special Mention in the White Ravens catalogue of the World's Best Children's Books in 2000. But just what is a grabooberry? Now that would be telling . . .

Bad Bad Cats

Roger McGough, illustrated by Lydia Monks

Puffin Books (1997) PB £4.99 ISBN: 0 14 038391 3

A collection of more than 70 hilarious poems about cats, but also featured here is an array of incredible characters such as an aristocratic and arrogant swan and even one about yourself as the 'Reader of this Poem'. There is also some useful and serious advice on how to stop alligators from biting your bottom when you are on the toilet and another one giving some sound advice for travellers, and even a poem that needs to be read lying down – 'A Weak Poem'. These are all short poems that can easily be read aloud in the classroom and using this collection will be a magnificent way of promoting poetry from an early age and associating poetry and reading with fun. Children will adore the poems featured in this volume and Lydia Monks' black-and-white illustrations marvellously interpret the text and add an extra dimension to each poem. McGough and Monks have collaborated on a number of other projects, some of which are featured in this publication.

The Bee's Knees

Roger McGough, illustrated by Helen Stephens
Puffin Books (2003) PB £4.99 ISBN: 0 14 131495 8

'The Opening Poem' is the first poem featured in this volume and it also aims to introduce the contents of the book. Be prepared to meet the most incredible characters and most outrageous situations: dancing pigs and puppy cats, glow rats and elephants on skis. Also imagine how would you feel if you became a book, or the pleasures experienced in having an imaginary friend. There are poems for every mood: 'Ten' is about a child who ponders about being ten years old and is full of nostalgic thoughts about his early years, gone and never to come back again. There is a clever composition about the Universe 'In Here and Out There' and the tale of a rat who wanted to glow in the night like fireflies and then ended up sheltering in a shed from the hungry owl. These are all poems that beautifully touch the spirit of childhood and are highly recommended as a first introduction to poetry.

The Book about Moomin, Mymble and Little My

Tove Jansson, translated by Sophie Hannah
Sort of Books (2005) HB £8.99
ISBN: 0 9535227 4 1

Who Will Comfort Toffle? A Tale of Moomin Valley

Tove Jansson, translated by Sophie Hannah
Sort Of Books (2003) HB £8.99
ISBN: 0 9535227 9 2

The Moomin books by Tove Jansson (1914-2001) are already contemporary classics of children's literature and they are usually available in fiction book format. These picture book versions are a total joy as the colourful, vibrant and highly original illustrations perfectly match the highly sophisticated novelty design. The cut-through hole pages in *The Book About Moomin, Mymble and Little My* create anticipation in the reader and together with the rhyming narrative succeed in bringing alive the story of Moomintrol who walks all alone through the dark woods and encounters Mymble who is very upset because she has lost her little sister My. As they search for little My they meet the most terrifying creatures.

In *Who Will Comfort Toffle?* we encounter Toffle who lives in a little house in the middle of the wood, but he is driven away from his home by the mysterious noises coming from the forest. On his journey he

meets many folk but he is too timid to talk to any of them and consequently feels very lonely. Until one day, by the seashore, he finds a message in a bottle from a girl called Miffle who is crying out for help. The book was first published in 1960 in Finland. Sophie Hannah's translation is witty and poetic enough to capture Jansson's own idiosyncratic voice. All the funny creatures in these stories are vividly brought to life by the glorious illustrations. This is a marvellous opportunity to introduce children to the pleasures of narrative verse. Both stories are magical, warm, very human and touching. Typography, design, illustration and musical text succeed in making these tales a memorable reading experience that children and grown-ups will want to revisit again and again.

Bring in the Holly

Charles Causley, illustrated by Lisa Kopper

FRANCES LINCOLN (2000) PB £5.99 ISBN: 0 7112 1571 5

A seasonal selection of 12 poems about Christmas by a winner of the Queen's Gold Medal for poetry, Charles Causley. This large-format, beautifully illustrated full-colour book would make a perfect gift. The collection contains poems on traditional Christian themes ('Mary's Song', 'Angels' Song') but takes a less reverent look at the festival too, through the eyes of Si-Si the siamese cat ('They're Fetching in Ivy and Holly') and the lament of a Christmas pudding. It also includes viewpoints from other European countries, with translations from the German and a description of celebrations in a provincial village. 'The Animals' Carol' provides an elegant introduction to Latin, incorporating various words and phrases for which an accompanying translation is worked into the verse. Classy, but unintimidating.

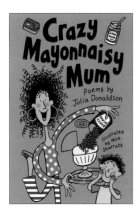

Crazy Mayonnaisy Mum

Julia Donaldson, illustrated by Nick Sharratt

MACMILLAN CHILDREN'S BOOKS (2004) PB £3.99 ISBN: 0 330 61690 9

Julia Donaldson is well known for her picture books including *The Gruffalo*. But she also had a career singing and song writing, mainly for children's television. Her verse shows the same perception and sense of fun as her books. Some of it almost seems to have a tune written into the words. This is a vibrant collection of story poems, noisy rhymes, a number sequence and more reflective poems. There are some short versions of Aesop's fables and some very funny observations of pet and family behaviour. The repetition in 'Walking the Dog' conveys a brilliant image of a dog's energetic racing around. These poems would be good to read aloud or alone. None of them is longer than a double page spread, including illustrations. They would engage anybody with their humour and pace. Nick Sharratt is also well known, as an illustrator (especially for Jacqueline Wilson) and a picture-book author. His black-and-white illustrations add to the lively, fast-paced feel of this collection.

The Crocodile is Coming

June Crebin, illustrated by Mini Grey

WALKER BOOKS (2005) PB £4.99 ISBN: 1 84418 965 6

Crebbin says in her introduction that she wanted to create a collection of poems of different shapes and sizes and I think she achieves that goal with aplomb. The only thing you can definitively say about all of them is that they all relate to the experience of being a child. There are numerous different forms of poetry here, some rhyming, some not. Crebbin shows once again that she is one of the best children's writers around. This would be an ideal book with which to introduce young children to reading poetry and also encourage them to produce their own. There are lots of ideas to draw from, such as writing a poem in a shape as Crebbin does in poems like 'Kite' and 'The Lolly's Last Request'. The expressive pictures, drawn by Mini Grey, add much to this book. They are exclusively black and white and are striking, charming and often amusing. Despite there being more than 50 poems within the book, it is a slim volume that would not be intimidating to a reluctant reader. Appealing, humorous and accessible, this is a superb collection for young children. Shortlisted for the CLPE Poetry Award 2006.

Daft as a Doughnut

Adrian Mitchell, illustrated by Tony Ross

ORCHARD BOOKS (2004) PB £4.99 ISBN: 1 84362 685 3

This is a hugely eclectic collection of poems on a range of themes, organised into sections such as 'Animals Forever', 'Magic Journeys', and 'Only Kidding'. It's wittily illustrated by Tony Ross, usually with several black and white pictures on each page. Adrian Mitchell, one of our finest and most accessible children's poets, has the knack of writing as if he is speaking directly into your ear. There's an intimacy and accessibility about these poems, which puts the poet on the same level as the reader. Mitchell's joy and enthusiasm are infectious. Sometimes his poems are humorous, and sometimes not, but either way, it's a simple matter to find your way into them. There are two delightful poems in the book dealing with the potentially vexed question of how to write a poem, but Mitchell truly leads by example, demonstrating multifarious ways of approaching all kinds of material. An inspirational collection that was shortlisted for the CLPE Poetry Award 2006.

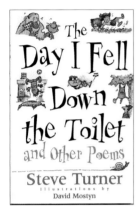

The Day I Fell Down the Toilet and Other Poems

Steve Turner, illustrated by David Mostyn

Lion Children's Books (1997) pb £4.99 isbn: 0 7459 3640 7

The poems in Steve Turner's collection are categorised under such headings as 'I Like Words' and 'Rhythm and Rhyme'. Through verse he explores the nature of words, their meanings and the way they sound. For example, in 'Bottoms' he ventures that bottoms are not at our bottoms at all but at our middle and so, more accurately, our feet should be called our bottoms: "Scuse me, you stood on my bottom / I must rest my bottoms awhile / Football would hardly be mentioned / As bottomball came into style". By taking an inquisitive, almost childlike approach to looking at words he is able to poke fun at the quirks of language. In 'It's Raining Cats and Dogs' words take on their literal meaning which leads to a macabre yet humorous scene. Under the heading 'Other Ways of Seeing Things' ordinary, everyday activities are turned on their heads. Poems answer questions such as 'Why can't we watch sandwiches and eat televisions?' And if you're one of those people who hate eating vegetables, the poem 'The Vegetables Strike Back' considers how it might feel to be the vegetable. However, this collection is not all humorous, light-hearted fun. More serious issues are dealt with in the section entitled 'Messages to the World'. Here poems provide children with topics to ponder on, looking at environmental damage, poverty and how to make the world a better place. Steve Turner's strong rhymes are complemented throughout by David Mostyn's amusing black-and-white illustrations.

Einstein: The Girl who Hated Maths

John Agard, illustrated by Satoshi Kitamura

HODDER CHILDREN'S BOOKS (2004) PB £4.99 ISBN: 0 7502 4288 4

If you have ever fought with fractions or diced with decimals, this extraordinary collection of unique poems about numbers is intended to engage and inspire. Acclaimed poet, John Agard uses rhyme to explore the world of Einstein, a girl who hates maths and loves cats: "Her parents liked the name / so they called her Einstein. / And how she hated maths. / She'd rather play with cats / Or do a drawing of the sunshine". As Einstein's cats begin to multiply, her number-loving parents gently encourage her conversion to mathematics. During this, the writer celebrates the beauty of bisectors and perfection of pi in poetry that amuses and informs. Here we discover why the number nine is special and how to travel the shortest distance between two points. Superbly illustrated with Kitamura's bold drawings and geometric shapes, this collection of humorous and thoughtful verse will appeal to both the numerically fascinated and the fearful.

Excuse Me, is this India?

Anushka Ravishankar, illustrated by Anita Leutwiler

TARA PUBLISHING (2003) HB £7.99 ISBN: 81 86211 56 X

The lilting, poetic text by Anushka Ravishankar is inspired by and woven around the exquisite quilt images by artist, Anita Leutwiler, who created pictures from the different fabrics she had collected during a trip to India. This is a story of a child's imaginary travels resulting from the stories that her Aunt Anna tells her while sewing a quilt full of pictures of the places she has been and the things that she has seen. "To warm me through winter she sewed me a quilt / With pictures of all the things she had seen". Every page has a different quilt image that takes the reader on a wonderful and colourful journey and readers are kept guessing as to where they are. The illustrations are vibrant with their striking colours and the style that echoes the old quilting forms in India which have traditionally held the women's memories of the past.

Fairy Poems

Clare Bevan, illustrated by Lara Jones

MACMILLAN CHILDREN'S BOOKS
(2005) PB £3.99 ISBN: 0 330 43352 0

More Fairy Poems

Clare Bevan, illustrated by Lara Jones

MACMILLAN CHILDREN'S BOOKS
(2005) PB £3.99 ISBN: 0 330 43935 9

Mermaid Poems

Clare Bevan, illustrated by Lara Jones

MACMILLAN CHILDREN'S BOOKS
(2005) PB £3.99 ISBN: 0 330 43785 2

Princess Poems

Clare Bevan, illustrated by Lara Jones

MACMILLAN CHILDREN'S BOOKS
(2005) PB £3.99 ISBN: 0 330 43789 X

As the titles suggest, these books are devoted to poems about mermaids, fairies and princesses. Each poem is preceded by a brief introduction, often explaining where the poet 'found' it – for example 'in the Wicked Queen's spell cupboard', or 'sent by sea-mail'. This mischievous spirit of fun continues throughout the books, which have sparkling, colourful covers, and pages decorated with stars and Lara Jones' amusing and childlike drawings. In Clare Bevan's books, the secret worlds we are let in on are both playful (with naughty fairies who have fun jumbling up your jigsaws, grumpy magic mirrors, and shells serving as mermaids' mobile phones) and also full of mystery: who saved the fisher lad from the sea; where is the source of the Fairy Queen's power; and how does Beauty reconcile her complex feelings about the Beast's home? The poems are largely formal in style and the collections include shape poems and acrostic poems, counting poems, riddles, and verse letters. It is easy to see the evidence of her declared admiration for another children's poet who wrote about mermaids, Charles Causley – Clare Bevan uses rhyme and metre with great accomplishment.

The poems will work best for those with a grounding in European folk and fairy tales, as many of them are inspired by and make direct references to these. These tastes of fairy tales should entice children to explore other versions of the stories that make up this rich tradition, and teachers to use the poems as a jumping-off place for the study of folk and fairy tales. However, the books are not always helpful in this direction: *Princess Poems* provides a 'Palace Glossary' to explain, for example, the story behind her poem 'The Twelve Dancing Princesses', but there is no reference to Hans Christian Andersen with relation to 'the Little Mermaid' poem.

Good Enough to Eat

Roger McGough, Illustrated by Lydia Monks

PUFFIN BOOKS (2002) PB £4.99 ISBN: 0 14 131494 X

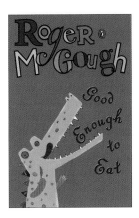

Whether it is for breakfast, lunch or dinner, here is a collection of poems good enough to eat at any time. The masterly, inventive crafts-manship of Roger McGough sprouts through this collection of funny, thought-provoking, original and inventive poems. 'The Boy with a Similar Name' is a poignant portrayal of a lad who is a bully and the pain he inflicts on his victim. 'Tea Leaves' tells of Mrs Lee who spends her evenings extracting information, not from books or magazines, but from tea leaves. Then we learn about the pleasure of reading and how the poet feels when he is trying to get inspiration for a new poem. In 'The Perfect Present' we can relate to the story, since what we want is not what we always get! The above are just a few examples of the wide range of poems in this book, which covers various topics from dreams to food and a tour around a bedroom. The poems are mostly very short but it is amazing how much an author can explore with just a few words. There are also two riddles (with answers provided at the end) and an index of first lines. Lydia Monks' black-and-white illustrations are expressive and have wonderfully interpreted the essence of each poem.

Guess What Happened at School Today

Jez Alborough

HARPERCOLLINS (2005) PB £5.99 ISBN: 0 00 713631 5

Set in a primary school, this collection captures a day in the life of Miss Chadwick's class. Each poem chronologically takes the reader through all the experience (good and bad) that the day has in store. In 'Are you supposed to be somewhere?' a boy gets lost in the hallway or in 'Miss Chadwick's in a mood today' the children wonder what could be making their teacher angry and in 'Joanna's got a horse called Ned' a girl rides her imaginary horse. Using a simple rhyming structure Jez Alborough has managed to evoke each giggle, fear, scraped knee, embarrassment and joy found in every playground. Bright, simple illustrations complement the verse, with a clock keeping time on each page.

If I Were a King, If I Were a Queen

Véronique Tadjo

MILET (2002) HB £7.99 ISBN: 1 84059 339 3

Tadjo's inspiring little book provides a variety of answers to the question of what to do if you're a royal, and young children will want to add plenty of their own ideas after reading it. The answers move from the initially selfish – "I would sit all day long / doing nothing / and drinking fresh coconut juice / in the shade" – to the more altruistic dreamers – "I would abolish poverty. / There would be no street children, / no more beggars". Each pronouncement is accompanied by colourful illustrations giving a child's-eye view of African Kings and Queens from Rwanda to Morocco. The message is uplifting and the perspectives offered will provide a refreshing antidote for children raised on fairytale visions of courts and castles.

I Heard it from Alice Zucchini:
Poems about the Garden

Juanita Havill, illustrated by Christine Davenier

CHRONICLE BOOKS (2006) HB £9.99 ISBN: 10 0 8118 3962 1

This delightful collection of 20 poems about the garden includes a lively 'Pea Pod Chant', a group of vegetables who go dancing to a club called the 'Vegetable Stew' and gossiping vegetables in 'Garden Gossip'. The reader can also take a wander through the Rhubarb Forest that is eventually baked in a pie in 'Nursery Rhyme' and there are poems about seedlings and instructions for planting as well. The longest poem in the book, called 'The Pumpkin's Revenge', is a poem about what happened to the pumpkin from the 'Cinderella' story and how he ended up in a Paris museum! Written by American author, Juanita Havill, the poems are accompanied by the magical watercolour illustrations of Christine Davenier. Beautifully laid out, this book about the garden will enchant children and delight gardeners of all ages.

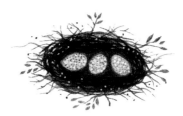

I was only Asking

Steve Turner, illustrated by Nigel Baines

LION CHILDREN'S BOOKS (2004) PB £4.99 ISBN: 0 7459 4822 7

The much-respected Steve Turner offers a collection of poems posing questions and musing on a wide range of curiosities and issues, including school, money, daydreaming, dressing up, discovering one's special talents, washing hands, telling lies, discerning the difference between right and wrong and even nose-picking! The collection is arranged according to type of question, the first section on the nature of questioning itself, then such questions as 'What Am I?', 'Who Am I?', 'Where Did I Come From?' and 'How Should I Live?'. Sometimes light-hearted, sometimes deeply serious, these wonderfully perceptive, humorous and philosophical reflections on the question of what it means to be alive are accessible as read-aloud poems for both older and younger children and as independent reading for older children, even those who are not enthusiastic about poetry. The accompanying black-and-white illustrations by Nigel Baines lend light-hearted animation to virtually every page. Although paperback, the binding is of good quality and should survive the repeated use this fine, thoughtful collection no doubt will receive.

Jumping the Waves: Sglod's Favourite Poems

Ruth Morgan, illustrated by Suzanne Carpenter

PONT BOOKS (2002) PB £4.95 ISBN: 1 84323 106 9

A collection for seaside holiday reading, this is a translation from the Welsh of Morgan's verse, which centres on the character of Sglod, a dog who lives at the chip shop on a pier in the fictional resort of Abertwt. Accompanied by collage-style pastel, paper and photo illustrations, Sglod's selection of his favourite poems covers every aspect of a holiday from gift shop goodies to sand, holiday snaps, sandwiches and chips. Many, but by no means all, of the poems are humorous and some of the simplest are the most effective. 'Shell' is a shell-shaped poem, beautifully illustrated by Carpenter, which spirals into an ellipsis: "Listen closely to my shell / oh what secrets it may tell . . .". Some of the verse plays with better-known models ("Twinkle twinkle little starfish") or forms a mnemonic from the town's name. There's even a poem in the shape of a lolly.

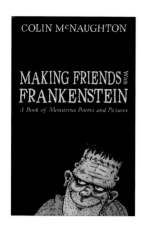

Making Friends with Frankenstein: A Book of Monstrous Poems and Pictures

Colin McNaughton

WALKER BOOKS, 2003 PB £4.99 ISBN: 0 7445 9666 1

The subject matter of this entertaining book of 56 poems about monsters ranges from headless phantoms and vampires to show-offs and sycophants. These can be quite grisly ("Wen I is ungry for me lunsh, it's hewmin beens I luvs ta crunch!") but any possible horror is usually offset by McNaughton's slapstick comedy and tongue-in-cheek lightness of touch. The humour can come from puns designed to make the youngest of readers groan ("ogre my dead body") as well as appealing silliness ("Have you noticed how the yeti / Rhymes so neatly with spaghetti?"). Many poems are perfect for reading aloud as McNaughton revels in onomatopoeic words ("Slobber, chomp, slurp, gulp!"). As McNaughton drew the illustrations while actually writing the poems they complement each other well. Although the original edition of the book was the winner of the 1993 British Book Design and Production Award, the book continues to be as fresh today as it was then and will amuse both children and those adults reading along with them. Perfect for monstrous children, and those who have to cope with them!

The Mighty Slide

Allan Ahlberg, illustrated by Charlotte Voake

PUFFIN BOOKS (1989) PB £4.99 ISBN: 0 14 032335 X

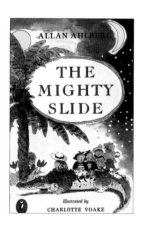

This is a collection of five stories in verse or narrative poems. 'The Mighty Slide', the title of the book, is about a group of adventurous school children who are sliding in the snowy playground. In 'Captain Jim', a child falls in the river and is threatened by very hungry and ferocious crocodiles until the courageous and mysterious Captain Jim triumphs by coming to the rescue. 'The Girl Who Doubled' tells the story of Alison Hubble "who went to bed single and woke up double". But the story does not end there as she keeps multiplying and soon there are hundreds of Alisons everywhere! 'A Pair of Sinners' is based on the Victorian crime of 'child stripping', where well-dressed children were accosted in the streets and robbed of their clothes. In Ahlberg's story, a sister and a brother are the thieves who mistakenly take the robes of the Prince of Wales and get jailed for their crime. The last of the stories is 'The Scariest Yet' where a teacher tells the pupils a scary story of two boys locked in a boiler room in a school during the Second World War. An amazing collection of stories with beautiful black-and-white line drawings by award-winning artist Charlotte Voake that perfectly capture the spirit of the tales.

The Monsters' Guide to Choosing a Pet

Roger McGough and Brian Patten, illustrated by
Guy Parker-Rees
PUFFIN BOOKS (2005) PB £6.99 ISBN: 0 141 31766 3

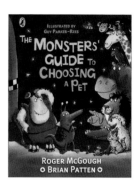

Two of Liverpool's favourite sons collaborate to create this grand array of animal- related poems. From conger eels to dogs, an amazing range of animals are celebrated in this imaginative collection. The poems are extremely accessible and entertaining and will appeal to many that may not be reading's keenest fans. One of the highlights is a revised version of 'The Teddy Bears' Picnic, US Flies in Hamburgers' which pokes fun at the fast food industry: "It's lovely down in MacDingles today / But if you don't fancy flies / Better I'd say to keep well away / Stay home and eat birds' eyes". The book is produced so it almost looks like a thick picture book, which leaves ample room for both the text and the expansive line drawings. There is a great sense of the visual within these pages shown by the innovative use of black. An enjoyable and entertaining read.

The Moon Has Written You a Poem: Poems to Read to Children on Moonlit Nights

José Jorge Letria, illustrated by André Letria
Translated from Portuguese by Maurice Riordan
WINGED CHARIOT PRESS (2005) HB £12.99 ISBN: 1 905341 00 8

This picture book from Portugal is a good example of how much the children's book publishing market has progressed and developed there over the last few years. It is an ideal book to read aloud and also for bedtime reading, as the poetic language is highly evocative and touching with a melodic flavour that perfectly suits its purpose. Any young child will fall asleep peaceful and serene after listening to the rhythmical sound of the words, travelling in their imagination to the fantastic places mentioned in the story; poems full of dreams, words with beautiful sounds, light and magic, all this is to be found here. José Jorge Letria invites the readers – or the listeners- to travel with their imagination to far away places. The surreal illustrations by André Letria are touching and full of mystery and fill the predominant part of the double-page spread. (This review first appeared in *Outside In: Children's Books in Translation* published by Milet).

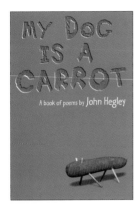

My Dog is a Carrot

John Hegley

WALKER BOOKS (2002) PB £5.99 ISBN: 0 7445 8633 X

This is one of the maddest, funniest, most colourful books ever encountered. John Hegley is one of England's most imaginative and exciting poets and this comes through in this marvellous collection, suitably titled *My Dog is a Carrot*. If your dog is not very doglike because it is orange and crunchy then this is the book for you. But if your dog is perfectly doglike you will still love these poems. Hegley's poems are full of energy, noise, squeals and squawks. They are often more like pictures than words, and the actual pictures add to the text and are also full of madness, oddity and colour. A typical example being the picture on page 14 of 'loggie' which illustrates 'A Comparison of Logs and Dogs'. Loggie is a log shaped like a dog. The book is luxuriously designed and produced and would make a great addition to anyone's bookcase.

Runny Babbit: A Billy Sook

Shel Silverstein

MARION BOYARS (2005) HB £8.99 ISBN: 0 7145 3300 9

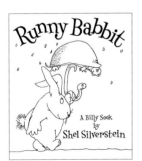

In this playful collection, published posthumously, Shel Silverstein explores the whimsical world of contradictions made up of spoonerisms, where the first parts of words are transposed as in this billy sook's title of *Runny Babbit*. Aiming at young children, the poet humorously observes many aspects of a child's life, from nose picking to making mud pies, through the topsy-turvy experiences of a mischievous but compassionate babbit. The tongue-twisters can be a mouthful but Silverstein's poems are clever and subtle, so that in reading each line the mind begins to put the letters back in their proper place. Although in essence light-hearted and suitable for very young chil dren (even under 5's), there is also a profound quality to this collection as seen in the tender 'Runny's Hand-New Brat'. Silverstein's verse is complemented by his trademark line drawings. This is a gorgeous and unforgettable compilation, which delights in the sheer pleasure of language and begs to be read aloud.

Smile, Please!

Tony Bradman, illustrated by Jean Baylis

PUFFIN BOOKS (1989) PB £4.99 ISBN: 0 140 32286 8

A simple, fun collection of verse about families, relationships and schooldays that should strike a chord with all primary-school children. There are rhymes to chime with most early life experiences, from the coming of a new sibling ("Can we have a gerbil, mum?" / "We can't," is what mum said. / "I'm sorry, love," she added, / "I'm having a baby, instead.") to the troubles of sharing a room, going on a school trip or being frightened by something on the telly. There are also some good experiments with what poems can be, and the shapes they make on the page – one follows a buzzing bee as it moves back and forth among the flowers; another mimics the rhythms of a football as it's kicked repeatedly against the wall. These, and others, make great starting places for playing word-games of your own.

Star in the Custard

Nicola Davies, illustrated by Elaine Franks

PONT BOOKS (2004) PB £4.99 ISBN: 1 84323 328 2

A slim collection of poems based around a Welsh family. Bethan and Gareth are twins, with two very different ways of looking at the world – a world that includes little brother Gwilym the Kid, adventurous grandparents, a dopy dog, a cat just finding its paws, and plenty of dressing-up clothes. The title poem refers to the words within words that make reading so difficult for beginners, while many of the others display a simple yet sophisticated and musical use of language. This is particularly true of 'Darkness', an evocative poem about a cat's solitary night times. Family life and imaginative play feature in equal parts, and many poems paint accurate and funny pictures of family life, expressed in easily memorable rhythmic verse. Franks' illustrations add an extra perceptive, funny, magical dimension to the verse, and help make this is an attractive and unusual themed collection.

Individual Collections

The Tail of the Trinosaur

Charles Causley, illustrated by Jill Gardiner

Jane Nissen Books (2006) PB £6.99 ISBN: 1 903252 23 7

It's wonderful to see that this classic narrative verse for children, by one of the most important British poets of his generation, has been published in this new edition by Jane Nissen Books. Charles Causley's hilarious story in rhyme is witty, sometimes irreverent, full of variety with its twists and turns in the story, as well as compassionate. After millions of years a Trinosaur is unearthed in the clay of the Amazon Jungle and sent as a gift to the peace-loving township of Dunsborough. When the articulated lorry arrives with a massive crate the townsfolk are in for one almighty shock! However, the Trinosaur herself turns out not to be a terrifying monster after all, but a loveable though somewhat clumsy vegetarian. Rich with its inventiveness of rhyme and rhythm, this is a book that needs to be read aloud. As Michael Rosen describes it in his introduction to the book: "Here is a virtuoso poem, full of delights, corners, originalities and surprises". This is not just a book that children will enjoy, but one that adults too will want to read again and again.

Taking out the Tigers

Brian Moses, illustrated by Chris Garbutt

Macmillan Children's Books (2005) BP £3.99 ISBN: 0 330 41797 5

In his postscript to this collection, poet and anthologist Brian Moses says that "many of the poems in this book were inspired by visits to different places". But the feelings expressed are not tied to a geographical location. There is awe and peace in the Alps in 'This Moment of Magic', improvisation and expectation in a Sussex back garden trying to emulate the Nevada Desert in 'The ET Runway' and even 'Hang-Gliding Over Active Volcanoes': "Yes, I got singed from my eyebrows to my toes, / I got scorched from my kneecaps to my nose / From hang-gliding over active volcanoes". There are poems inspired by his visits to schools and museums and verses on teachers, pupils, animals and outer space. It is a funny, thought-provoking new collection that inspires and entertains. The black-and-white stylised cartoon illustrations by Chris Garbutt suit the mood of the poems. They have a 1950's retro look, but it fits the whole production.

Today is MY day

Anushka Ravishankar, illustrated by Piet Grobler

TARA PUBLISHING (2003) HB £7.99 ISBN: 81 86211 76 4

Tala is fed up with people always telling her what to do. Everyone orders her around: her parents, teachers, sisters and classmates. Most of the time she usually listens to them – "But not today!/ No, not today / For TODAY IS MY DAY" – and no one can tell her what to do! This is a wonderful nonsense verse from Anushka Ravishankar that follows Tala's day as she sets out to make it her own in the most unusual way. The quirky illustrations by Piet Grobler portray Tala's fiery independent spirit as she fights to make the day hers. The clever use of typography with its different size and shape of letters and words on the page, together with the rich colours of black, red and white helps to enhance the verse. A beautifully produced book from India that is ideal to share aloud.

The Tortoise Had a Mighty Roar

Peter Dixon, illustrated by David Thomas

MACMILLAN CHILDREN'S BOOKS (2005) PB £4.99 ISBN: 0 330 41799 1

With nearly a dozen previous poetry books to his credit, Dixon is well known in the classroom and library for his varied verse, his sense of humour and the serious undertone to some of his work. This collection is no exception to that general rule, and includes poems on private and public occasions, stories from legends and the Bible, and on the things that go wrong (and right) at school and at home, and how we deal with them. A slim volume, sympathetically illustrated, as are many of Dixon's books, by David Thomas. This will attract older readers, and provide a useful resource for reading aloud to classes of this age and slightly older. There are several poems which will cast fresh light on common problems encountered at this age, many of which are summed up in the thoughtful poem 'I Am'. Readers will also recognize many of the excuses given in the poem of that name!

Watch Out for Sprouts!

Simon Bartram

TEMPLAR (2005) HB £9.99 ISBN: 1 84011 368 5

Simon Bartram is probably better known as artist and illustrator and for his outstanding picture books like *The Man on the Moon* and *Dougal's Deep-Sea Diary*. *Watch Out for Sprouts!* is a welcome debut as a poet and he has succeeded in creating a hilarious collection of verse with topics that range from the various types of sausages that can be found, to the autobiographical account of a poet's writing block. Included in this compilation is a funny poem of a toilet with teeth, a comparison of childhood days in the 1960s and a captivating description of were-wolves and hippies, just to mention a few. 'I'm Off to see the Queen' has to be the winner of them all: imagine you are invited to the Palace, what would you wear? What present would you take? Would you get there on time? Praise also needs to be given to his colourful illustra-tions that are a strong mark of his unique and distinctive style, and to the appealing design and typography. Finally, there is also some advice from Simon Bartram himself to all those aspiring poets: "to write poetry all you need is a reliable pen".

We are Britain!

Benjamin Zephaniah, photographs by Prodeepta Das

FRANCES LINCOLN (2003) BP £5.99 ISBN: 0 7112 1902 8

The talented Benjamin Zephaniah has collaborated with photogra-pher Prodeepta Das and a fine design team at Frances Lincoln to pro-duce this bright visual and lyrical celebration of the multicultural face of modern British youth. A short preface by Zephaniah intro-duces thirteen children from throughout the British Isles, both urban and rural settings, and discusses the notion that children from very different ethnic, cultural and regional backgrounds are all still British and in fact define what it now means to be British. Each spread offers a brief factual portrait of a British young person, accompanied by photographs and a rhyming poem inspired by the personality and life-style of the child. Zephaniah's rhythmic poems about hard-working Kenny from a farming family in Scotland, for example, or confident, pizza-loving Jajar from a Sikh immigrant family in Essex, paint a colourful picture of the variety of backgrounds of modern British youth. Although the poems might not quite reach the high standard of Zephaniah's previous works of poetry for children, the celebratory spirit of the book and its excellent production make it a worthy addition to any poetry collection. The playful, multi-coloured graphics and layout of text and photos complement the book's emphasis on joyful diversity and help to bring to life these thirteen lovely children.

When We Were Very Young

A. A. Milne, illustrated by

E. H. Shephard

EGMONT CHILDREN'S BOOKS (2004)
PB £6.99 ISBN: 1 4052 1118 0

Now We Are Six

A. A. Milne, illustrated by

E. H. Shephard

EGMONT CHILDREN'S BOOKS (2004)
PB £6.99 ISBN: 1 4052 1119 9

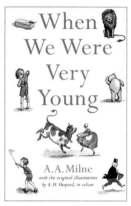

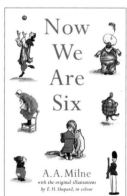

A book of reviews of children's poetry would not be complete without these two timeless classics by A. A Milne which constitute some of the most familiar poetry in the English Language, with many adults remembering them from their own childhood. Favourites like 'Halfway Down' – "Halfway down the stairs / Is a stair / Where I sit. / There isn't any / Other stair / Quite like / It", 'Buckingham Palace' where "Christopher Robin went down with Alice" or 'Jonathan Jo' who had a mouth like an 'O', the King's partiality to butter in 'The King's Breakfast' or 'The Dormouse and the Doctor', about a dormouse who lived in a bed of delphiniums (blue) and geraniums (red) are just a few of those unforgettable and unmissable poems.

Now We Are Six is the second volume, with Christopher Robin a little older and the now renowned Winnie-the-Pooh appearing in many more of the verses. In 'Us Two' they are inseparable: "Wherever I am, there's always Pooh, / There's always Pooh and Me". More amusing verse follows about bad King John in 'King John's Christmas' or Christopher Robin as he lies ill in bed in 'Sneezles' or the King of Peru in 'The Emperor's Rhyme'. Two all-time favourites that all young children will appreciate. With the distinctive, inimitable illustrations of E. H. Shepard, no childhood would be complete without these wonderful books of verse.

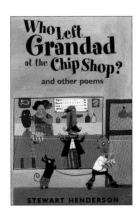

Who Left Grandad at the Chip Shop? and other poems

Stewart Henderson

LION CHILDREN'S BOOKS (2002) PB £4.99 ISBN: 0 7459 4551 1

With a colourful cover, high quality paper, compelling line drawings and an intriguing title, this book by poet and Radio 4 regular Stewart Henderson has all the ingredients necessary to attract the reader. It is divided into different 'worlds' within each of which the poems are thematically linked. 'Me and my World' deals with school and family, 'Water World' includes poems about whales, goldfish and washing machines, while 'Imaginary World' includes a poem about what may or may not live behind the skirting board, and one in the tradition of Ted Hughes' *Meet My Folks!* about 'Auntie Diluvian' who 'goes quiet' when it rains and 'Uncle Orang' who passes his time 'peacefully sucking his fleas'. The section about 'Just a Mo the Eskimo', however, may seem rather out of place in a time when other poetry books for children explore different cultures in a more developed way. Repetition, rhyme and rhythm drive the poems. The tight shorter poems are particularly successful and work well when read aloud. This strong use of repetition and rhyme also makes *Who Left Grandad at the Chip Shop?* a good book to help develop confidence in young readers.

Wish You Were Here

Anushka Ravishankar, illustrated by various artists

TARA PUBLISHING (2003) HB £7.99 ISBN: 81 86211 75 6

Absurdist-verse specialist Ravishankar has produced a quirky collection of postcard poems from a very peculiar family. Grandpa Laung has fallen off the Eiffel Tower, Uncle Tettra Hedran has moved into an Egyptian pyramid and Aunt Parapetta has gone to climb the Great Wall of China. Each postcard finds its way home to the armchair-bound narrator, who prefers a cushioned chair to wandering here and there. All the locations have been illustrated by commercial poster artists, and include 'snapshots' of the various bug-eyed family members. Entertaining and upbeat, this would make a fun starting-point for children wanting to try composing a 'postcard poem' of their own.

Aliens Stole My Underpants and Other Intergalactic Poems

Edited by Brian Moses, illustrated by Lucy Maddison

MACMILLAN CHILDREN'S BOOKS (2004) PB £3.99 ISBN: 0 330 43874 3

An omnibus edition of two of Moses' earlier selections, with almost 50 poems about aliens and space travel, mainly humorous, and also illustrated with many suitably quirky cartoon pictures. For newly confident readers, a great advantage of poetry anthologies over fiction is the slimness of the volumes, the limited length of many poems, and the aid which rhythm and rhyme can give to word recognition. Even at double its previous size, this small paperback is ideal for the older readers in this age group and beyond to dip in to. Although these are poems about unfamiliar and imaginary people and places, precisely because they focus on the differences between these and our planet and its inhabitants, their effect is to make readers think about their own appearance, habits, behaviour and experience. It is also an ideal starting point for creating words and poems of their own, with the 'DIY UFO Poem' supplying several hundred words in three columns which can be easily put together into countless three-word lines.

All the Colours of the Earth

Selected by Wendy Cooling, illustrated by Sheila Moxley

FRANCES LINCOLN (2004) HB £12.99 ISBN: 1 84507 014 3

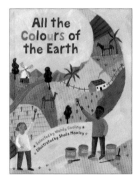

From the arresting world of vibrant colour portrayed in Sheila Moxley's illustrations, to the personalised notes on the poets, this anthology provides a thought-provoking reading experience for children. Wendy Cooling explains in her introduction that the poems "show what children share as well as reflecting the differences in their lives". The book achieves this through juxtaposing poems with similar themes by poets from different cultures and different periods. Paper boats, kites, and swings are familiar to Indian, British, Jamaican and Maori children alike. Whether in a Caribbean market or an American supermarket, the colours and variety of produce can be bewildering. But children's experiences include working all day picking through rubbish dumps, as described so poignantly in Gloria Guevara's poem, one of a number of translations in the book. The final poem, Benjamin Zephaniah's 'Good Hope' reflects the spirit and message of this uplifting anthology: "I know/ Every day / Children cry for water . . . Still every day / Children play / With no care for colour".

A Twist in the Tale

Chosen by Valerie Bloom

MACMILLAN CHILDREN'S BOOKS (2005) PB £4.99 ISBN: 0 330 39899 7

Each poem in this anthology is characterised by its unexpected ending. Included are irreverent re-workings of traditional fairy tales such as 'The Tale of the Ugly Duckling' by Marianne Chipperfield, 'Cinderella's Revenge' by Kaye Umansky and 'Beauty-Sleeping' by Jennifer Curry, where the happily-ever-after endings are given a cheeky twist. It's not all fairy tales though, in this quirky collection of verse. Find out what happened to the girl whose parents said she could moan for England and so entered her in a regional heat, and discover what happened to the invisible boy who went to school naked. Also featured are poems dealing with aliens, embarrassing dads and the trials of having younger siblings. The form of the poems ranges from long narrative rhyme to short limerick-style verse: "A cynical man from Mauritius / Thought it foolish to be superstitious / When a black cat passed near / He stood firm without fear / . . . What a shame the panther was vicious". Full of dry humour and featuring a selection of multicultural verse, this varied collection of poetry is sure to surprise and amuse.

Best Friends

Chosen by Fiona Waters, illustrated by Michael Broad

MACMILLAN CHILDREN'S BOOKS (2006) PB £3.99 ISBN: 0 330 43789 5

Fiona Waters is the anthologist of over 20 books of poetry for children. For *Best Friends*, she has chosen poems about a wide variety of aspects of friendship. This anthology explores the pleasure derived from having a friend, and the intense pain that can come from a rift, the responsibilities friendship brings with it, and the loneliness of being without a friend. While the majority of these poems (mostly by contemporary writers for children) are about friendships with peers, poems about pets and about positive relationships with parents and grandparents are also included, and imaginary friends make an appearance too. The wide-eyed characters in Michael Broad's illustrations are sympathetic and engaging. While the illustrations and the cover design might suggest that this book is aimed primarily at girls, the content by no means precludes a male audience. With its focus on the emotions engendered by friendship, *Best Friends* will help its readers negotiate the challenges of their own relationships.

The Carnival of the Animals

Poems inspired by Saint-Saëns' Music,
illustrated by Satoshi Kitamura

WALKER BOOKS (2005) HB £10.99 ISBN: 1 84428 021 7

This enchanting collection successfully combines the three different art forms of language, art and music to provide a magical selection of specially commissioned work from some well-known contemporary poets including James Berry, Kit Wright, Adrian Mitchell, Charles Causley and Valerie Bloom. The inspiration is the music of the celebrated French composer Camille Saint-Saëns, who wrote the 'zoological fantasy' that has become popular as a piece of classical music for children, although he regarded it as 'too frivolous' and allowed only 'Le Cygne' to be published in his lifetime. The eleven contributors wrote a variety of different poems about animals to tie in with the music. James Berry's poem about the 'Lion' and Adrian Mitchell's 'Elephant Eternity' evoke the beauty of these magnificent creatures while poems like Kit Wright's ' Cocks and Hens' and Gerard Benson's 'Personages With Long Ears' keep you amused. With the vibrant illustrations by Satoshi Kitamura perfectly matching the text, this is a very special collection of poetry. An accompanying CD of the poets Cicely Herbert and Gerard Benson reading the poems to music, followed by the music itself, provides nearly one hour of listening. Shortlisted for the CLPE Poetry Award 2006.

The Dog Ate My Buspass

Chosen by Nick Toczek and Andrew Fusek Peters,
illustrated by Axel Sheffler

MACMILLAN CHILDREN'S BOOKS (2004) PB £3.99 ISBN: 0 330 41800 9

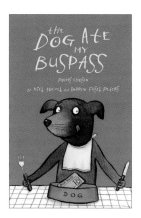

Nick Toczek and Andrew Fusek Peters give new meaning to the theme of elaborate excuses in this engaging and amusing compendium of skillfully chosen poems of apologies, fibs and excuses. The volume's 58 poems, some brief, some lengthy, some free verse, some rhymed, are all equally provocative. There are poems about locking up a younger sibling in a shed and savouring the act despite getting caught, about why the cow didn't jump over the moon, why the wolf ate Little Red Riding Hood, about a washing machine's antics with laundry, a list of the worst excuses in the world, the runaway contents of a late poem, a cloud's excuse for causing rain – in short an excuse in verse for just about everything. The talented Alex Sheffler lends his skill to virtually

every page with black-and-white illustrations that make the poems all the more provocative. Adults will marvel at just how much mischief can be contained in one small volume, while children will not manage to control the impish gleam of understanding that each poem inspires.

The Elements of Poetry

Compiled by Andrew Fusek Peters

EVANS BROTHERS (2006) HB £9.99

FIRE   ISBN: 0237 528851
WATER   ISBN: 0237 52886X
EARTH   ISBN: 0237 528878
AIR   ISBN: 0237 528886

The Elements of Poetry is an exciting new series of collections of poetry about the elements – Fire, Water, Earth and Air – compiled by well-known poet and anthologist, Andrew Fusek Peters. Each book contains over 20 poems in a diverse mix of different forms and styles ranging from classic to contemporary.

Fire has poems about candles for the festivals of Hanukkah and Diwali, bonfires, flames, volcanoes and a poem in the shape of the Sun. Two poems, one modern, one classic, describe the terrible events of the Great Fire of London in Eric Finney's 'The Great Fire' and an extract from 'The Fire of London 1666' by John Dryden, an eye-witness account. *Water* has poems about drought, ice, fog, waterfalls, rainbows, the sea, rain and floods, while Tony Mitton's 'Voices of Water' explains what water is. Two very contrasting poems by Polly Peters highlights how crucial water is to all of us. 'Girl 13, Malawi' tells of her twenty-minute walk to collect two buckets of filthy water that are subsequently boiled and used for drinking, washing and cooking and that results in making her brother sick, while 'Girl, 13, UK' demonstrates how water is taken for granted in the West.

Earth shows how important worms are for the soil in 'Don't Tread on Worms!' while the powerful poem, 'Earth', deals with the destruction of the land. Poems about the Amazon, desert, gravity, mountains and earthquakes are also featured here together with Jane Clarke's poem in the shape of a spider's web that looks at how we are all part of the great worldwide 'Web of Life'. *Air* has poems about wind, thunder, lightning and balloons together with poems in the shape of human lungs and a tornado. An explanation of the different categories of hurricane is to be found in 'Wind Forces – The Beaufort Scale' by Doda Smith and Philip Waddell's 'If, All of a Sudden, Air Wasn't There' provides an explanation of what would happen if we didn't have air. These are four fine collections of poetry and are an ideal way of learning about the elements, as well as providing a perfect cross-over between literature and science. They are clearly laid out, with stunning photographs adorning each page.

Fiendishly Funny Poems

Picked by John Foster, illustrated by Nathan Reed
COLLINS (2004) PB £3.99 ISBN: 0 00 714803 8

Completely Crazy Poems

Picked by John Foster, illustrated by Nathan Reed
COLLINS (2003) PB £3.99 ISBN: 0 00 714802 X

Seriously Scary Poems

Picked by John Foster, illustrated by Nathan Reed
COLLINS (2003) PB £3.99 ISBN: 0 00 714801 1

Fiendishly Funny Poems has you laughing all the time with such ridiculous rhymes as 'E-pet-aph' by Andrew Fusek Peters and Polly Peters about Gerry the gerbil who got trapped in the trouser press and was pressed in peace or the dad with a hole in his hair, 'My Dad' by Pat Gadsby. When the in-spectres turned up at school it didn't quite go according to plan in 'The Inspection' by Rachel Rooney, as the behaviour of the pupils simply wasn't bad enough! 'Builder's Bum' is an amusing take on the traditional rhyme 'Monday's Child' ("Monday's child has builder's bum. / Tuesday's child has a rumbly tum") and 'A Glance At the Menu' is a nonsense rhyme about vegetables dressing up by Richard Edwards.

Crazy Poems is a completely zany set of nonsense poems. The rattlesnakes are having a knees-up 'At the Hop', by Anne Logan, 'The Toilet Seat Has Teeth' has the bathroom going crazy in a poem by Paul Cookson and there is a new kind of gravy that hovers and drifts about with ease and "You'll puzzle over how to pour it / neatly on your peas" in 'Anti-gravity Gravy' by Tony Mitton, while 'The Toffee Mine' by Michael Comyns turns out to be a very sticky affair.

In *Seriously Scary Poems* you can hear 'The Werewolf's Howl' by Wes

Magee, experience 'The Fear' by Brian Moses or be trapped by 'Locks', a poem in the shape of a lock: "They lock you in so without a doubt, / take great care or you'll never get out!". All three anthologies by John Foster are complemented by comic black-and-white line drawings by Nathan Read which are guaranteed to provide lots of amusement.

If the Sea Was in the Sky . . .: Poetry Collection 5

Compiled by Fiona Waters, illustrated by Tracy Fennell

EVANS BROTHERS (2002) HB £6.99 ISBN: 0 237 52126 1

An enjoyable poetry collection for young children compiled by Fiona Waters. It offers a kaleidoscope of poems both new and old that are full of magic, mystery and humour. There are poems about family and friends, nature and animals, ghosts and other mythical creatures, words, dreams, with something for just about everyone. Poems about the family include poems on 'Mum' and 'Dad' by Andrew Fusek Peters and Polly Peters – mum is the "Sadness stealer" while dad is the "Tall-story weaver". Valerie Bloom's lyrical poem about 'Frost' contrasts with an amusing poem about a lion who becomes vegetarian in 'The "Veggie" Lion' by Spike Milligan: "Now I just eat carrots, / They're easier to Kill, / Cos when I pounce upon them, / They all remain quite still!" Richard Edwards' 'Don't' poem about why people say 'don't' so much will resonate with any child. Colourful illustrations by Tracy Fennell make this an ideal collection for reading aloud.

I Love My Mum

Chosen by Gaby Morgan, illustrated by Jane Eccles

MACMILLAN CHILDREN'S BOOKS (2006) PB £3.99 ISBN: 0 330 44102 7

This endearing collection of poems was published in March 2006 in time for Mothering Sunday, but the sentiments expressed are appropriate all year round. The magic of mums is the inspiration behind each poem; tribute is paid to the many things they do and the roles they fulfil: cook, teacher, agony aunt, best friend, role model, the list is endless. There is work by well-known names such as Julia Donaldson and Paul Cookson as well as some charming poems penned by children themselves, one poet as young as six. Whilst many of the poems take a fun, humorous approach to mothers and motherhood others are far more thoughtful and personal which results in a good mix of moods. Whether light-hearted or serious, each poem touches on the special relationship between mother and child. And the concept of motherhood is not just considered from a one-dimensional viewpoint; rather, experiences of motherhood from across cultures are included as well as experiences of foster mothers, stepmothers, and grandmothers. This collection is a celebration of multitasking, multitalented, selfless mums and a great reference point for children who wish to write their own poem for their mum.

The King's Pyjamas: A Poetry Collection

Compiled by Pie Corbett, Illustrated by Christopher Corr

BELITHA PRESS (2003) PB £6.99 ISBN: 1 84138 767 3

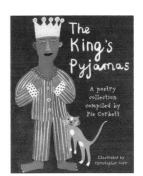

This anthology of verse contains more than 50 poems on a wide variety of topics, organised under headings such as 'My friends and family', 'Time for School' and 'Weather and Wonder'. The illustrations, in full colour, are vivid and appealing and the choice of poets is representative of the huge range of writers creating poetry for children today. Most of the chosen writers are British, though there are a few Americans, but Corbett eschews, for the most part, the obvious, over-anthologised pieces in favour of work by younger, lesser-known writers. That said, there are still some old favourites here from Edward Lear to Brian Patten and John Agard. The approach is accessible and fun. There is advice on how to answer irritating questions about growing up, how to get your granny out of bed and the answer to the mystery of what happens to teachers when the kids go home at the end of the day.

Let the Sun Shine: A Read Aloud Collection

Chosen by Kaye Webb, illustrated by various artists

FRANCES LINCOLN (1998) PB £5.99 ISBN: 0 7112 1247 3

Kaye Webb, founder of the Puffin Club, was an expert anthologist, and this selection of poetry and prose, originally published more than ten years ago, bears witness to her art. Its original title, *Round About Six*, indicates the age group for which she made her choice, and it remains an unbeatable selection for readers of this age group and those slightly older. Its attraction and use is far beyond the classroom, however, as this is a wonderful picture book which should feature on every child's bookshelf. The quality and variety of authors represented, among them Charles Causley, Betsy Byars, and Margaret Mahy, is matched by the illustrators of this edition – including Tony Ross, Quentin Blake, Jan Pieńkowski and Nigel Baynes – each splendidly individual and well suited to each other. Webb's selection of stories and poems is ideal for adults to use as end of the school day or bedtime reading, and will surely encourage young (and grown-up) readers to investigate further both the authors and illustrators represented here.

Monster Poems

Brian Moses, illustrated by Axel Scheffler

MACMILLAN (2005) PB £3.99 ISBN: 0 33042048 8

This compilation of monster poems chosen by Brian Moses and illustrated by Alex Scheffler is great, in fact it's MONSTER-TASTIC! The reader is greeted on the front cover by a rather ferocious looking green monster (probably a cousin of The Gruffalo). Inside, the reader will find sensitive poems like 'Song of the Lonely Monster' and the hilarious 'King Kong's Car Boot Sale' and 'The Loch Ness Monster's School Report.' *Monster Poems* is a really enjoyable read from start to finish. Like monsters, the poems vary in length, some short, some long, and each one unique. You will never look at monsters in the same way again and, like Moses, you'll always remember to check under your bed before you go to sleep – you never know what might be lurking there…

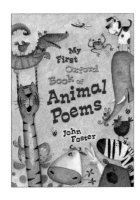

My First Oxford Book of Animal Poems

Compiled by John Foster, illustrated by various artists

OXFORD UNIVERSITY PRESS (2005) PB £7.99 ISBN: 0 19 276326 1

This anthology contains over 90 animal poems beautifully illustrated in colour by seven different artists. 'The Animal Alphabet' poem by John Mole at the beginning of the book sets the tone for this wonderful selection of poetry, including both classic and contemporary. All sorts of animals are featured here, from pets to insects, farm animals to sea creatures and beasts of the jungle. The poems about pets include 'The Song of the Mischievous Dog' by Dylan Thomas and 'Cats' by

Eleanor Farjeon. For the insects and animals living underground there is the delightful 'Spin Me a Web Spider' by Charles Causley, 'Tell Me, Little Woodworm' by Christopher Morley and 'The Mole' by Dick King-Smith. Judith Nicholls does an amusing take on one of Aesop's Fables with the 'Tortoise and Hare Poem (or: Slow, slow, quick, quick slow . . .)'. The book ends appropriately with the 'Song of the Ark' by Jack Ousby. Children will love the variety and humour in this anthology.

Never Say Boo to a Ghost

Chosen by John Foster, illustrated by Korky Paul

OXFORD UNIVERSITY PRESS (2004) PB £4.99 ISBN 0 19 276310 5

John Foster and Korky Paul's successful poetry partnership began in 1990 with the publication of this book which has gone on to sell over 100,000 copies. Here you will find poems to chill your bones and make you laugh at the same time. 'Voice of the Night' by Joan Poulson deals with a child's fear of the night and what it might bring as they listen in the silence for any sound, while imagining the appearance of some terrible vampire or ghost. There are amusing poems such as 'The Vampire's Wedding' by Marian Swinger and Charles Thomson or the series of advertisements by a Headless giant, an Easy-going Ogre and a Young-at-heart Ghost in 'Small Ads' by Colin West. Read about the ball at Grange Hall where there is a true ghost party taking place or the tale of the junior ghost who is frightened with a 'Boo' and ends up in disgrace in Margaret Porter's 'Never Say Boo to a Ghost'. The combination of John Foster's witty selection of poems and Korky Paul's zany, imaginative illustrations makes this book ideal for introducing young children to poetry.

Poems to Annoy Your Parents!

Chosen by Susie Gibbs, illustrated by Jess Mikhail

OXFORD UNIVERSITY PRESS (2003) PB £4.99 ISBN: 0 19 276290 7

Poems to Freak Out Your Teachers!

Chosen by Susie Gibbs, illustrated by Jess Mikhail

OXFORD UNIVERSITY PRESS (2003) PB £4.99 ISBN: 0 19 276292 3

These two anthologies of poems chosen by Susie Gibbs are guaranteed to make you laugh but also think. In *Poems to Annoy Your Parents!* there are poems about children trying to get out of going to bed or cleaning their

room, in 'If you make Me Go To Bed Now' by Jeff Moss or 'Sick of Socks' by Liz Walker, but also a more serious poem by Jackie Kay about a fraught relationship with parents called 'Divorce' and the beautiful poem 'Tiger' by Hilaire Belloc. *Poems to Freak Out Your Teachers!* has hilarious verses on how to impress your new teacher, a sponsored silence or 'The Inspector Calls' by Gervase Phinn that is highly unlikely to impress any inspector! There are some limericks and a very ingenious poem about turning the tables on teachers, with a pupil taking over the running of the school in 'I Dreamt I Took Over . . .' by Trevor Millum, and to end the book Allan Ahlberg's delightful 'Teacher's Prayer'. These two books feature a fantastic array of traditional and modern poems. With fresh, stylish illustrations from Jess Mikhail, this collection will appeal to anyone who likes a good chuckle.

The Puffin Book of Nonsense Verse

Selected and illustrated by Quentin Blake

PUFFIN BOOKS (1996) PB £6.99 ISBN: 0 14 036660 1

The Mad Hatter, a friendly cinnamon bun and the Jumblies all collide in this lively anthology. The legendary Quentin Blake has not only assembled an assortment of the finest nonsense verse from the likes of Hilaire Belloc and Edward Lear but also illustrated them with his trademark line drawings. From the limericks of Spike Milligan to the ballads of Lewis Carroll, Blake's artistic contributions delightfully capture the tone and mood of the rhymes. This sensational selection not only celebrates the classic rhymes of Ogden Nash and A. E. Houseman, but also treats us to the contemporary poems of Roger McGough and Shel Silverstein. Surreal and silly, this engaging and eclectic collection of nonsense verse is extremely accessible. It will encourage children to appreciate the humour poetry can create.

The Secret Lives of Teachers: Revealing Rhymes

Chosen by Brian Moses,
illustrated by Lucy Maddison and Tim Archbold

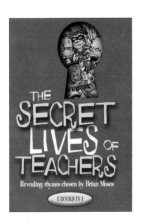

MACMILLAN CHILDREN'S BOOK (2005) PB £4.99 ISBN 0 330 43282 6

The mystique of the teacher lives on! Children are forever fascinated with their teachers. We all remember our teachers; we spent countless hours concocting all kinds of fantasy stories about them. *The Secret Lives of Teachers* will provide an endless source of amusement. Some of these poems were recently read to a Year 4 class – their particular favourites included 'Miss Rose Lee', 'Bogeyman Headmaster' and 'Tea', but the book is jam-packed with poems and 'revealing' rhymes to answer every pupil's questions such as, is Sir a secret agent? what goes on behind the staffroom door? and does my teacher *really* live at school? These 'revealing rhymes' are a real treat.

Silly Poems
Compiled by Paul Cookson, illustrated by Sarah Naylor

SCHOLASTIC CHILDREN'S BOOKS (2005) PB £3.99 ISBN: 0 439 95981 0

Magic Poems
Compiled by Jennifer Curry, illustrated by Philip Hopman

SCHOLASTIC CHILDREN'S BOOKS (2003) PB £3.99 ISBN: 0 439 97761 4

Silly Poems is a compilation by poet and anthologist, Paul Cookson. With riddles, tongue twisters, haiku, clerihews, epitaphs, nursery rhymes, limericks, jokes, puns, nonsense verse and wordplay, there is certainly enough for the reader to choose from. Try the tongue-twister, 'Twong Tister' ("six slim slender saplings") by Clive Webster, or the 'Naughty Acrostic' riddle by Paul Cookson. Meet the rapping haiku or the 'Four Soccer Clerihews' and an amazing alphabet in 'An Alphabet of Alphabeastical Facts' with iguanas who can't rollerskate and penguins who can't use telephones.

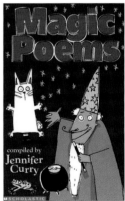

Magic Poems is another sparkling poetry collection from anthologist, Jennifer Curry, which includes work by well-known poets such as Tony Mitton, Judith Nicholls and John Foster. There is the broomstick that has a mind of its own in 'Broomstick Obedience Class' and is eventually turned into a vaccum cleaner by its exasperated owner, or 'The Preston Witch' who suffered from acute indigestion. 'Magic Cat' sees some spilt magic on the floor that results in all sorts of strange mishaps, not least of which is the turning of mum into a snail, dad into a mouse and the narrator into an ant, while the cat takes over the house! These two books are part of a series of poetry collections from Scholastic and they are sure to provide hours of entertainment. Look out for the other titles: *Animal Poems, Disgusting Poems, Family Poems, Funny Poems, Pet Poems, School Poems* and *Spooky Poems.*

Space Poems

Chosen by Gaby Morgan, illustrated by Jane Eccles

MACMILLAN CHILDREN'S BOOKS (2006) PB £3.99 ISBN: 0 330 44057 8

This is a brilliantly simple looking collection. The pages are unclut-
tered, with plenty of white space. The choice of font, short straightforward poems and plentiful black-and-white line illustrations all invite
beginner readers to attempt these verses for themelves. There are poems
from many contemporary authors such as Paul Cookson, Brian Moses
and Gareth Owen, on all aspects of space – rockets, space travel, aliens,
planets and stars and even space pets! Just because they are easy to read,
doesn't mean they don't provide thoughtful imagery, as, for example
in Wendy Cope's 'Where am I?' riddle poem describing the moon and
Gareth Owen's description of a grandfather and grandson's loving imaginative play in 'Shed in Space'. There are shape poems and a few
science facts but mostly it's imagination that takes us to the stars.

Trick or Treat

Chosen by Paul Cookson, illustrated by David Parkins

MACMILLAN CHILDREN'S BOOKS (2005) PB £3.99 ISBN: 0 330 42630 3

Another selection by Paul Cookson of petrifying poems which have all
the right ingredients to make a perfect Halloween. There are instructions on how to make a Halloween pie, as well as all the Halloween traditions; Marian Swinger's skeletons doing 'trick or treat', especially in
wellington boots in 'Skeletons in Wellingtons'; and how a real ghost is
turned away 'At the Halloween Party' and "left in a huff / when they
told it its costume / was not good enough" or the major mishap caused
by 'The Broomstick That Wouldn't Fly!' in Ian Bland's poem; all these
will all provide endless amusement. There are plenty of scary poems
too, such as Trevor Millum's 'So Dark' or 'The Invisible Man' by John
Mole. Accompanied by David Parkins' black-and-white illustrations
this collection is sure to be an ideal choice for Halloween.

The Trying Flapeze
and Other Puzzle Poems

Compiled by John Foster, illustrated by Tony Ross

OXFORD UNIVERSITY PRESS (2004) PB £4.99 ISBN: 0 19 276314 8

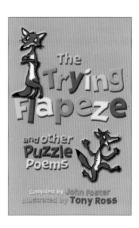

In this engrossing selection of puzzle poems the reader will find anagrams, anagriddles, crosswords, inside-out words, hidden words and much, much more. The title poem, Liz Brownlee's 'The Trying Flapeze', has young Raymond writing a postcard to his parents full of spoonerisms after a nasty flying trapeze accident. There is a reflection poem, an upside-down poem and a punctuation poem as well as text, maze and number poems. Hieroglyphs are used in 'The Lost Pharaoh' by Richard Caley; Melissa Lawrence's 'A Lipogram' is a poem in which one letter of the alphabet is not used and in the delicious 'Hidden Chocolate' poem by Pam Gidney we are asked to drool while identifying all the chocolate mentioned! The back of the book contains answers to the various puzzle poems. This is an original and unusual approach to poetry that will appeal to a wide variety of readers.

The Universal Vacuum Cleaner
and Other Riddle Poems

Compiled by John Foster, illustrated by Tony Ross

OXFORD UNIVERSITY PRESS (2005) PB £4.99 ISBN: 0 19 276313 X

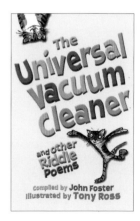

This is another absorbing collection by John Foster of 52 riddle poems that include haiku, mystery riddles, riddles with hidden words, and much more. There are many riddles that keep readers guessing, including Clare Bevan's 'Santa's Mystery Letters', a riddle poem of four letters written by various animals to Father Christmas with the reader having to guess the identity of the authors, a shape poem, 'What Is He?' by Liz Brownlee and 'What Book Am I?' by Debjani Chatterjee. There is the amusing 'Crumbs' riddle by Roger Stevens and the 'Riddle for the Teacher' by Granville Lawson. This collection of riddle poems will provide hours of entertainment for anyone who enjoys puzzling and word-games, as well as being a highly satisfying anthology of cleverly conceived poetry. Amusing black-and-white line drawings by Tony Ross accompany the riddles.

Walking The Bridge Of Your Nose: Wordplay Rhyme Poems

Selected by Michael Rosen, illustrated by Chloë Cheese

KINGFISHER (1997) £8.99 ISBN: 0 7534 0149 5

This book is an unfettered celebration of language. It consists of contemporary and traditional tongue-twisters, plenty of rebuses that will be a challenge even to a texting generation, nonsense poetry, experimentation with punctuation, riddles, puns and parodies. The text is imaginatively set within brightly coloured illustrations by Chloë Cheese. These often provide the key to the more puzzling wordplay. For those riddles that still prove too tough a challenge, there is a list of answers at the back of the book. While some readers might have appreciated explanations of the different forms of wordplay, others may feel that it is cracking their codes independently that gives most satisfaction. For on every page you will find not only a giggle, as Michael Rosen warns in his introduction, but also a route into language, and a sense of its possibilities. Readers will be desperate to share these poems with anyone willing to listen!

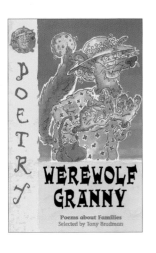

Werewolf Granny: Poems about Families

Selected by Tony Bradman, illustrated by Colin Paine

BLOOMSBURY CHILDREN'S BOOKS (1999) PB £3.99 ISBN: 0 7475 4468 7

This richly varied collection will be particularly enjoyed by this age group, although an older group would appreciate it too. These are not all new poems; Stevie Smith's work can be found here, as can Eleanor Farjeon's, along with that of more contemporary writers like Tony Bradman and Valerie Bloom. The poems are stylistically varied; you'll find free verse and metred verse side by side, some of it humorous, some serious: the short ironic poem by Paul Bright, 'Brotherly Love', which ends with the couplet "If I saw you only yearly / I'd adore you, yours sincerely", is very funny, whereas 'Divorce', by Mike Jubb, has a much more sombre tone. There are plenty of entertaining black-and-white illustrations. A nicely judged, inclusive anthology of poems where most children will find something, or someone, to identify with. The subject matter is broad and the approaches are varied; subjects like death and divorce are dealt with sympathetically and truthfully. It would stimulate any young reader to think about their own family and the place they themselves have in an increasingly complex world of relationships, but always from an imaginative and positive perspective.

Word Whirls and Other Shape Poems

Compiled by John Foster, illustrated by Clare Hamstock

OXFORD UNIVERSITY PRESS (2005) PB £4.99 ISBN: 0 19 279156 7

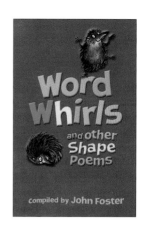

Here are an absorbing, whirling collection of shape poems set out under eight different themes including animals, nature, food, fun and games, word smatterings and the human body. The poems come in all shapes and sizes and this is a unique feature of each poem. You will find poems in the shape of a giraffe, a hippopotamus and a seahorse. 'Breakfast' by Noel Petty sees dad reading the newspaper and 'Filtered Magic' by Trevor Harvey appears in the shape of a coffee maker. Wes Magee provides 'The Twenty Steps to the Cellar' and Trevor Millum presents 'The Letter that was Never Sent'. Then there is Gina Douthwaite's poem in the shape of the human body, 'Bodies', and the clever 'Pylons' by Christine Morton. This book will provide hours of entertainment for anyone who enjoys visual puzzles and games.

Alligator Pie

Dennis Lee, illustrated by Frank Newfeld

KPK BOOKS (2001) HB £9.99 ISBN: 1 55263 338 1

This witty Canadian children's classic was written in 1974 by Dennis Lee and contains a selection of wonderful playful rhymes in a variety of styles. There are some fun nursery rhymes at the beginning of the book for younger children – 'Singa Songa', 'Bouncing Song' and 'Mumbo Jumbo' – moving on to nonsense verse for older children, such as the 'Rattlesnake Skipping Song', about the brown-bread-eating rattlesnakes of Mississauga, a 'Tongue Twister', 'Like a Giant in a Towel', 'On Tuesdays I Polish my Uncle', or the story of Beatrix Potter's 'Peter Rabbit' in rhyme and 'The Sitter and the Butter and the Better Batter Fritter'. The rhymes are accompanied by bold, vibrantly colourful illustrations, which enhance the humour of the text. Children will not fail to be amused by this array of zany nonsensical rhymes which are ideal for reading aloud.

All Things Weird and Wonderful

Stewart Henderson, illustrated by Nigel Baines

LION CHILDREN'S BOOKS (2004) PB £4.99 ISBN: 0 7459 4898 7

The weird and the wonderful are indeed well represented in Stewart Henderson's lyrical ruminations on the natural world. Arranged according to the world above, around and below us, Henderson's poems are short and accessible yet thoughtful and thought-provoking. In 'And now the zoos are empty', he writes of the consequences of liberating animals from the zoo. In parallel poems, a girl sends a prayer to her animal soulmates, the elephants, and receives a warm reply. In another poem, a three-legged mongrel wins a dog competition, and in yet another, the alphabetical order of animal names in a dictionary creates a new natural order. The cartoon-like black-and-white illustrations by Nigel Baines and the volume's cover design and title encourage a headlong dive into these capricious and clever poems.

A Pizza the Size of the Sun

Jack Prelutsky, illustrated by James Stevenson

COLLINS (2003) PB £4.99 ISBN: 0 00 713999 3

It's Raining Pigs and Noodles

Jack Prelutsky, illustrated by James Stevenson

COLLINS (2003) PB £4.99 ISBN: 0 00 713998 5

A Pizza the Size of the Sun is a wonderfully rich and witty collection from one of America's funniest poets. Meet 'Miss Misinformation' who is completely full of nonsense and 'Quentin Quimble Quamble Quayle', the unrepentant tattletale who cannot resist telling tales or repeating secrets, or the maddeningly frenetic 'Frenetica Fluntz' who does so many things all at once. The grumpy old man in 'I Do Not Like the Sunshine' will annoy you and meeting Reverso, in 'Reverso Is Name My' will just confuse you since he does everything in reverse! You will also find out what is on offer at 'Gloppe's Soup Shop', who is at 'The Improbable Emporium', why Dan is the invisible man and wrestling with an octopus is really not a good idea. As well as all the wacky poems there are some serious ones too, such as the contemplative 'When I Am Full of Silence'.

It's Raining Pigs and Noodles is another fine collection of over 100 outrageously funny poems. There's the incredibly dirty 'Grungy Grace' or some tasty things to eat in 'Percy's Perfect Pies' such as delicious "Apple Cappuccini Rat" or "Skunk Asparagus Supreme". In 'I Took a Sip of Water' the drinker continues to expand as he drinks more and more water only to discover that it was not a good idea to eat so many sponges. In this crazy world you can also find the residents of 'Bumble by the Bay', hapless Peter who turns into a parking meter in 'See What Happened' ("On the curb he stands all day, / wishing dogs would go away"), and watch out for something nasty lurking 'Deep in Our Refrigerator'. A more serious poem is 'We Are Plooters', about those who are content to destroy and pollute wherever they go. Both these completely off-the-wall collections are accompanied by black-and-white illustrations by James Stevenson.

Bairn Rhymes:
Scots Verse for Children

J. K. Annand, illustrated by Dennis Carabine

MERCAT PRESS (2006) PB £7.99 ISBN: 1 873644 85 X

J. K. Annand was born in Edinburgh and these poems are steeped in the Scottish idiom. This book contains the poems from the three collections he published for children during his lifetime. Here are poems on many subjects from animals and birds to dentists and fishing boats, sparingly but vividly illustrated. Of course it would be easiest for Scottish children to understand the content; nevertheless, these poems are worth a second look: the music of the verses comes through loud and clear even if it's not immediately obvious exactly what they're about. The poet's ear was a finely tuned one, and the beautiful sounds of the language mean that the more you read, the more enjoyable it becomes. This collection could help children to focus foremost on rhythm and rhyme before content, which is a different and useful approach to poetry appreciation.

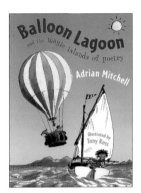

Balloon Lagoon and the Magic Islands of Poetry

Adrian Mitchell, illustrated by Tony Ross

ORCHARD BOOKS (2002) PB £7.99 ISBN: 1 84121 856 1

This is a lively collection in which Adrian Mitchell supplies the poems and Tony Ross the illustrations. It is a perfect match. Mitchell is interested in the humorous and imaginative possibilities of words and word combinations, while Ross is the master of the humorous line, inspiring the imagination with his economy. From the moment the anthology opens, the reader is transported into a world of the imagination. We are sailing on a lagoon with islands of poems whose names are as imaginative and fun as the works that inhabit them, Here is Mysteriosa, full of poems of wonder and strangeness – try 'The Woman of Water' or 'Mesopotamia' – or 'Iceberg Academy' for poems recalling familiar moments at school. This collection has been designed with a young audience firmly in mind and will demolish any idea that poetry is esoteric or only about 'proper subjects'.

Breaking the Rules and Other Poems

Coral Rumble, illustrated by Nigel Baines

LION CHILDREN'S BOOKS (2004) PB £4.99 ISBN: 0 7459 4857 X

This is a varied and wide-ranging collection that describes the world from a child's perspective. Here are poems about school and teachers, about loneliness and loss, about bullies and animals. Some are concrete poems and some are humorous, but not all. The black-and-white illustrations are fun and will help to keep young readers interested. The main strength of this collection rests in the subject matter. Many of the free verse poems lack a deeply coherent music, whilst the more formal ones are perhaps a little loose in their rhythmic structure. But the material is full of heart, strongly felt, the use of imagery is powerful and many of the ideas are quirkily expressed. The clearly delineated child's perspective makes them very accessible. They would make excellent jumping-off points for young writers exploring their feelings about certain issues or life experiences.

Can We Have Our Ball Back Please?

Gareth Owen, illustrated by Mike Phillips

MACMILLAN CHILDREN'S BOOKS (2006) PB £3.99 ISBN: 0 330 44048 9

This is a collection of football-themed poems by lifetime obsessive Gareth Owen. The book's subject matter and the relatively small volume can be an excellent way of getting previously reluctant boys to enjoy poetry. The poems cover all aspects of the beautiful game from playing in the street or ('The Commentator') or being a mascot for the local team ('Mascot') to playing Subbuteo ('Table Football'). Owen also explores football from the spectator's angle. His long-established love of soccer leaps vividly off the page and can be seen from those poems which pay homage to his childhood heroes as well as verses that chart the fortunes of his beloved Everton. Mostly metrically regular, the poems have rhymes that trip off the tongue and can be enjoyed equally by both listeners and readers. The shortest verse is only three lines ("Two-Four-Six-Eight, / Who do I appreciate? / Er me?") which means it is easy to find a suitable poem to read regardless of time constraints. Mike Phillips' line drawings accompanying them beautifully complement Owen's journey through the highs and lows of football.

Cat Among the Pigeons

Kit Wright, illustrated by Posy Simmonds

PUFFIN BOOKS (1989) PB £4.99 ISBN: 0 14 032367 8

Singing potatoes, mad dinner ladies and zoobs – everyday topics for a Kit Wright poem. Wright's tone has been described as kindly quirky humour, but this over-simplifies the underlying message of some of his work. This classic collection includes some sad and reflective poems such as 'Something He Left', which poignantly describes the coat left hanging in a wardrobe after "his body had gone / To be made into flame and memory", and put there on the night before "he put death on". Posy Simmond's powerful illustration for this poem imbues the coat with the personality of the dead man, retaining his shape even when empty. 'Finbar' describes the other end of life, how a frosty day is warmed by the birth of a tiny new life, while 'Mothering' considers the dichotomy of a life taken to feed another young life. Many of Wright's poems will encourage imitation and rhythmic experimentation, and all are eminently suitable for reading aloud.

Centrally Heated Knickers

Michael Rosen, illustrated by Harry Horse

PUFFIN BOOKS (2000) PB £4.99 ISBN: 0 14 130671 8

The *Star* (Science, Technology and Reading) Group asked Michael Rosen to write 100 poems about Chemistry, Physics, the Environment, and Design and Technology; the result is *Centrally Heated Knickers*. The book is divided into four sections featuring various facets of the above subjects. This is a marvellous way of introducing children to science in an enjoyable and funky way. Written in his inimitable style Rosen's poems are crying out to be read aloud whether to the individual child or to a group of children. There are plenty of things to learn from this collection of poems, which are not in any way pedagogic or educational. The intention being that of entertaining the audience and making young readers identify with certain situations and events as well as reflecting and widening their imagination. In 'Chocolate' a little boy proudly takes home some chocolate from a party, which melts in his hands. "Is this still chocolate?" he asks. In the poem, 'Pouring' it asks, "can we pour a teapot"? Or in 'Grandma's Hand' we discover that on a cold day rubbing your hands will keep them warm. These are just a few of the daily situations and events featured in this hilarious collection of poems.

Collected Poems for Children

Ted Hughes, illustrated by Raymond Briggs

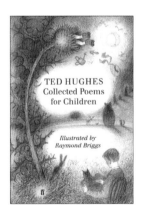

FABER AND FABER (2005) HB £16.99 ISBN: 0 571 21501 7

This Ted Hughes collection features poems written throughout his career. It is set out in volumes, organised according to age. The poems for the youngest are first and these could be read by an adventurous seven-year-old. The more sophisticated poems are towards the back of the book and these are aimed at an older crowd. All the poems can be enjoyed even as an adult as a result of Hughes' beautiful and funny style. He is never patronising or dull and the subject matter is a lot more varied than is sometimes the case with children's anthologies. Hughes writes knowledgeably and movingly of the natural world, as particularly in the poems from 'Collected Animal Poems: What is the Truth?' where he captures the essence of animals such as the hare, the fox, and the weasel. One of the highlights of this collection, however, is not Ted Hughes but Raymond Briggs. The cover on its own is enough to make you pick up the book, with its evocative twilight scene. The illustrations on the inside, all black and white line drawings, are placed so that they are almost part of the poetry, weaving through and around the text.

Dragons!

Nick Toczek, illustrated by Sally Townsend

Macmillan Children's Books (2005) PB £4.99 ISBN: 0 330 43744 5

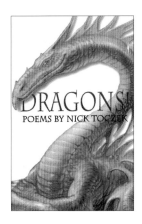

Nick Toczek unites fantasy with reality in a convincing and charming way in this collection of dragon-related poems. The very first poem in the collection demonstrates this, combining a very normal everyday dream that most school kids have, that school will be cancelled through some random calamity, with the extreme fantasy that the dragon will be that calamity and thus the student's heroine. There are other poems in the book, however, that are fantasy, such as 'Story-telling': "So knights are sent, huge muscled males / Who've rescued maids and hunted grails". With rhyme a very important feature, the poems lend themselves to being read aloud. The pictures are extremely detailed and lifelike. Any dragon lover would devour this collection with gusto.

The Emperor's Watchmaker

Lemn Sissay, illustrated by Gail Newey

Bloomsbury (2000) PB £3.99 ISBN: 0 7475 4755 6

A first children's collection from a brilliant poet, illustrated with line drawings throughout. The volume is loosely themed around the central character of an emperor, his palace and his staff. Sissay's verse sparkles with life and is great to read aloud. Strong rhythms and a sense of humour dominate. Meet the broken biscuit thief, the ghost who makes breakfast and the prince of toffee. There are shape poems – the circular 'Roundabout Roundabout' – and excuse poems ("when you don't want to go to the toilet"). The birds of the palace library should persuade even the most reluctant of readers: "The books in the library are folded birds. / They will raise you higher than you could imagine".

Everybody Got a Gift

Grace Nichols, illustrated by Rosemary Woods

A & C Black (2006) bp £6.99 isbn: 0 7136 7251 x

A collection of poems bringing together new poems with a selection previously published in some of Nichols' earlier books. The attractively spacious layout on fine paper is reflected in the higher cost of this small paperback over many other editions of poetry, which tend to value content over appearance. Nichols' poetry is vibrant, funny, deep and serious. Several of the poems are written in her native Guyanese dialect, inspired by her early childhood in the countryside and adolescence in the city. She also draws on her later British life to produce a collection which celebrates aspects of the two cultures, particularly the world around us and the people in it, and how we react to them. Nichols excels in creating vivid pictures in the reader's head with a minimum of words, and readers even encounter rapping babies and cats. Along the way she addresses death, deforestation and pollution, but it is the vibrancy and diversity of language which first takes our attention, before its deeper messages make us think beyond the words. A source of great inspiration for readers and thinkers.

Friendly Matches

Allan Ahlberg, illustrated by Fritz Wegner

Puffin Books (2002) pb £4.99 isbn: 0 141 30749 8

Allan Ahlberg's talent for picking up on the details of life and making his readers laugh is second to none. The poems in this diverse collection of football poems are in turn funny, moving, celebratory and contemplative, wholly appealing to football fans and non-football fans alike. This is a superb collection covering a range of different aspects of the game – referees, team talk, 1966 World Cup and more. There are poems to cater for every taste in relation to this popular sport: the little boy who is ill in bed and tries to persuade his mum to let him go out and join his friends playing football in the street in 'The Grey Boys, the 'Elephants v. Insects' football match; we can even discover that referees, despite facing lots of problems on the football pitch, can have fun in their lives in 'The Song of the Referee'. Written in a variety of verse forms – sonnets, rhyming couplets and narrative poems – and supported by Fritz Wegner's appealing artwork, this is a book that will not disappoint fans of previous Ahlberg collections such as *Heard it in the Playground* and *Please Mrs Butler*, both of which are also featured in *Universal Verse*.

The Frog who dreamed she was an Opera Singer

Jackie Kay, illustrated by Sue Williams

BLOOMSBURY CHILDREN'S BOOKS (1998) PB £3.99 ISBN: 0 7475 3866 2

Winner of the 1999 Signal Poetry Award, this atmospherically illustrated collection of Kay's poems for children crams a great variety of thought into a very small space. In her poetry Kay is particularly empathetic to those who find life crowding in on them because of their background or circumstances, and she voices the cries of the 'Stressed Out', the 'No-Speaks' and the 'Chatterbox', 'The Sick Bed', and 'The Past', in which she speaks for those who feel themselves inexorably changing. Her own mixed ancestry gives rise to 'At Home, Abroad' in which she searches for a feeling of identity, which also underlies the title poem. Kay's language also reflects her Scottish upbringing. This thoughtful book poses many of life's unanswerable questions, and Kay's intriguing exploration of their problems will appeal to the 9-11 age group as well as to older readers.

Funky Chickens

Benjamin Zephaniah

PUFFIN BOOKS (1997) PB £4-99 ISBN: 0 140 37945 2

This is the second collection of poetry for children by performance poet, Benjamin Zephaniah. His poetry is challenging, evocative and cool. Reading *Funky Chickens* is like reading rap, it seems immediate and makes you want to give the text voice and read it aloud. In fact it makes you want to jump about and shout. The subject matter varies hugely, from football to sewage. The tone is also unpredictable, veering from funny to serious and back again in a flash. Many have messages but they are not preachy or patronising, trying (successfully) to get the reader to think about important issues such as racism. The book itself is pleasingly produced with collage illustrations that remind one of Monty Python. A diverse and interesting collection guaranteed to get a reaction.

Gargling with Jelly

Brian Patten, illustrated by Chris Riddell

Puffin Books (2003) PB £4.99 ISBN: 0 141 31650 0

There is much to enjoy in this vibrant collection from one of Britain's most dynamic and enduring poets. Patten's trademark lyrical verse explores the surreal, comic, and serious in this most engaging compilation of children's poetry. His writing gives voice to an array of captivating characters from Cousin Lesley with his see-through stomach to Billy Dreamer's fantastic friends. The range of themes is equally diverse, from the sweetness of 'Squeezes' to the pathos of 'Burying the Dog in the Garden'. Chris Riddell's quirky illustrations both capture and complement the poet's clever rhymes. In 'The School Caretaker' it is as much Riddell's line drawing as Patten's verse that brings both the man and the monster to life. Here is a superb assortment of poetry that mixes the amusing with the melancholy in a collection which will engage and stimulate the imagination of children.

Ghostly Riders

Phil Carradice, illustrated by Maggy Roberts

Pont Books (2002) PB £4.95 1 84323 088 7

Using traditional verse forms in terms of rhythms and rhyme, Carradice writes about subjects that will appeal to young readers. He groups his poems under four headings: 'Spooky' – perhaps the most conventional in subject and handling, but also the ones that might grab the attention first; then the 'Family' – here a more bittersweet emotion creeps in (try 'When Granny Died'), among some rather obvious humour; the final two sections, 'History Jig-Saw' and 'All the year round', take moments from Welsh history and aspects of the countryside for their subject matter. These are the most successful poems – not for any great originality but because there is a real sense of personal engagement and observation that gives them immediacy and life. The Roman Soldier is a real person; 'On Dowlais Top' describes life in the iron smelting towns economically and effectively while there is a catchy simplicity to 'The best thing in the world' that brings the collection to a happy close.

The Good Child's Guide to Rock'n'Roll

Carol Ann Duffy, illustrated by Emily Feaver

FABER AND FABER (2003) HB £12.99 ISBN: 0 571 21455 X

With poems such as this collection of 'secrets and spells, songs of unrequited love, confessions and pleas' ranging from the Loch Ness Monster to Henrietta the Eighth, Duffy has become as well-known for her prose and poetry for children as she is for her writing for adults, and this latest book proves that she goes from strength to strength. Dedicated to her eleven-year-old daughter, it is ideally suited to this age group and older readers. The title work has sections on some of the major figures of rock'n'roll, many poems using lyrics from their best-known songs as refrains. Often using the rhythms of pop music, Duffy uses words with an energetic concision, in an incisive compression of thought and expression. She suggests more in a few words than many writers could in several hundred, and part of the challenge in reading her work is unpicking the layers to arrive at the core of her opinion. Much of this is serious, sophisticated stuff, but accessible at a great variety of levels, and eminently readable out loud.

Heard It in the Playground

Allan Ahlberg, illustrated by Fritz Wegner

PUFFIN BOOKS (1991) PB £4.99 ISBN: 0 14 032824 6

Illustrated by Fritz Wegner

This collection of amazing and humorous school poems was the result of the author spending a year in and out of Inglehurst Junior School, which is acknowledged in the book itself. Ahlberg gained inspiration from spending hours listening to children in the school playground, in assembly or lessons. The volume is divided into three sections: 'Short Poems', 'Songs' and 'Long Ones'. There are so many memorable poems in this book: 'Parents' Evening', in particular, captures not just the feelings of a young pupil scared and uncertain, but also those of the parents and the teacher. In another poem we all can sympathise and identify with the feelings expressed by a teacher and how each day she feels daunted by the challenges of her work in 'The Mrs Butler Blues'. This poem is featured in the chapter of songs, which means that it has the added bonus of being suitable to sing along to the tune if you are adventurous enough to do so. The volume forms an indispensable complement to the other classic *Please Mrs Butler*. Fritz Wegner's enchantingly detailed and precise black-and-white drawings bring the events alive.

Hello H₂0

John Agard, illustrated by Satoshi Kitamura

HODDER CHILDREN'S BOOKS (2004) ISBN: 0 340 89383 4

Hello H₂0 is a great teaching tool for home and school – imagine using the poem 'Two of One' to start a classroom debate on the issues of cloning or the haunting 'Who'll Save Dying Man?' to evoke questions on extinction and the theory of evolution. Pouring out from every page are poems that provoke and help to answer questions about the mysteries and complexities of our universe: Condensation? What's a Watt and who was he? Concave or convex? DNA – what do those letters stand for? Is there such a thing as moonlight? *Hello H₂0* is no flick through, dip in, dip out poetry book, it is so engaging that you will want to read it from cover to cover in one sitting. Imaginative, informative, well-researched and a lot of fun – an absolute must-have for the classroom to complement the Science curriculum.

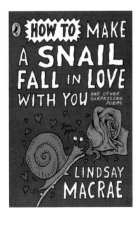

How to Make a Snail Fall in Love With You

Lindsay Macrae, illustrated by Steven Appleby

PUFFIN BOOKS (2003) PB £4.99 ISBN: 0 14 131430 3

Perhaps the book of poetry with the highest number of euphemisms for farting, and the only poem about seducing a snail, Lindsay Macrae's third collection of poetry for children also includes poems on autism, fair trade and divorce, as well as the children's poetry staples of embarrassing parents and irritable teachers. It explores wordplay and parody, contains very short pieces and longer poem sequences. Steven Appleby's cartoons, complete with his trademark sardonic annotations, perfectly illustrate the excruciatingly embarrassing Dad of the opening poem, the competitively disgusting blue-eyed monster, and the smugly satisfied Jane who has achieved two whole weeks in bed. The book also makes an attractive use of typographical variations. Font sizes and styles change to emphasise the poems' messages. While individual poems certainly hold great appeal, the collection as a whole perhaps lacks coherence. There are a bewildering number of subjects and styles here, each of which deserves more room to develop than this book can afford.

The Iron Man

Ted Hughes, illustrated by Andrew Davidson

FABER AND FABER (1989) PB £4.99 ISBN: 0 571 14149 8

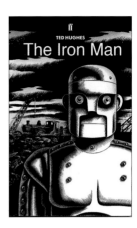

A novel amongst the poetry books? Why? Because this is a classic text, a modern fairy tale by a major twentieth-century poet, in which his mastery of language seamlessly brings poetry into his prose. Hughes describes an Iron Man, his head as big as a dustbin, his chest the size of a cattle truck, his arms like cranes, who is devouring the tractors, the fences and the ploughs. Mankind must put a stop to the dreadful destruction and set a trap for him, but he cannot be kept down. But when a terrible monster from outer space threatens to lay waste to the planet, it is the Iron Man who finds a way to save the world, and turn the threat into eternal peace. Hughes wrote several subsequent volumes of poetry for children, but this tiny novel is filled with an incredibly imaginative and powerful language, which is as poetic as anything he ever wrote. It provides an excellent point of comparison with Hughes' poetry, and advocates the power of a poet's viewpoint within prose.

Juggling with Gerbils

Brian Patten, illustrated by Chris Riddell

PUFFIN BOOKS (2000) PB £4.99 ISBN: 0 141 30478 2

Here is another gem of a collection from the master of lyrical verse for children, Brian Patten. Shortlisted for the Blue Peter Children's Book Award, *Juggling with Gerbils* explores the hilarious, serious, ordinary and bizarre in a compilation where nothing is quite what it appears. The poet's accomplished touch can make us chuckle at the boy with his finger stuck up his nose and at the same time weep for 'The Boy Who Broke Things': "The boy tore the curtain that separated life from death, / And so he could no longer tell / What was alive inside him and what was dead". Brian Patten is a clever and accessible poet who is able to take a common theme and turn it on its head, thus making the familiar seem absurd. This is complemented by Chris Riddell's skilful line drawings that express and enhance Patten's verse. Engaging and fun, this collection not only juggles with Gerbils but also probes the depths of a child's imagination.

Laughter is an Egg

John Agard, illustrated by Alan Rowe

PUFFIN BOOKS (1990) PB £4.99 ISBN: 0 140 34072 6

An acclaimed writer for both adults and children, Agard explores the meaning of laughter in this varied and bittersweet volume. He employs every possible verse form here, from raps, chants, riddles and haiku to spells, prayers, playlets and ballads. There's a healthy multiplicity of voices here, too, with Agard using Caribbean speech patterns and rhythms in many of the pieces; "Look at de sun / look at de moon / That's why / God got a yellow eye". Though many of the poems are playful and funny, he is not afraid to be serious as well: "To the house of the dead / Laughter will return". It's impossible to read his 'Spell to bring a Smile' without success: "Come down Rainbow / Rainbow come down / I have a space for you / in my small face". A very happy-making read, right down to the humorous black-and-white illustrations.

The Mermaid's Purse

Ted Hughes, illustrated by Flora McDonnell

FABER AND FABER (1999) PB £4.99 ISBN: 0 571 19621 7

In this short and sweet collection of poetry Ted Hughes offers us a real taste of the sea. He gives voice to an array of marine characters: a charming octopus luring seamen into the ocean depths, a wistful starfish gazing up at the stars in the night sky longing to be amongst them, and not forgetting the unfortunate mermaid who opened her purse only to unleash a hungry shark. The mood of the poems ranges from slow and melancholy to quirky and upbeat as in 'Jellyfish': "Though I look like a slob / It's a delicate job / Being a blob". Beautifully packaged, its sea-green cover gives way to black-and-white illustrations on every page, depicting at times the wildness of the sea and at others the sea's eerie stillness. No aspect of ocean life is too large or small to be included in this collection. From a majestic whale to a pebble, all are worthy of contemplation in this gem of a book that undulates throughout with the rhythm of the sea: "The sailors prayed to come to land / And their good ship's wreck soon made it, / And sat on the rocks like a one-man band / While the stormy sea still played it." ('Wreck').

Michael Rosen's Book of Nonsense

Michael Rosen, illustrated by Claire Mackie

HODDER CHILDREN'S BOOKS (2004) PB £6.99 ISBN: 0 340 89416 4

Michael Rosen in his element, delighting in rhymes, rhythms, word-play and sheer idiocy! These are poems to get young readers interested not only in the subject matter – whatever that might be, as it's all nonsense – but also in the possibility of playing around with words for themselves. There are more than 30 poems here which will make adults and children alike think about language, and why words mean one thing and not another – as Rosen says in his introduction this is not a potato, it's a book, and therefore it's not full of sandwiches, it's full of words. He delights in pointing out the nonsensical results when words are used in different contexts (for example jeans and Jean's), and thereby sets his readers thinking imaginatively. The limericks are a particular delight, and will encourage readers to experiment with this satisfyingly bizarre genre. Clare Mackie's colourful illustrations have just the right degree of lunacy about them, and she and Rosen have clearly collaborated closely to integrate word and picture. No self-respecting school library should be without this nonsense.

The Monster That Ate The Universe

Roger Stevens, illustrated by Jane Eccles

MACMILLAN CHILDREN'S BOOKS (2004) PB £4.99 ISBN: 0 330 41523 9

Roger Stevens' second collection of poems for children opens with the lines "Roll up, roll up / Get your poems here / They're lovely". The poems that follow confirm this delight in poetry and language. Readers are introduced to the many different forms and genres of poetry, and poems allude to the work of some classic poets for children. Poems like 'The Poetry Grand National' transmit and encourage an enthusiasm for poetic devices and language: "Halfway round the course / And Hyperbole is gaining on the leaders / Travelling at a million miles an hour". Gleeful conceits such as the family beach holiday in the back garden, the insatiable monster whose eating habits are progressively more extreme, and the less attractive openings in the superhero job market, make this appear at first to be a book of poems given over entirely to light-hearted fun. But the reader will come upon poems such as 'Farewell', 'Best Friend' and 'Grandma's Jigsaw Puzzle' that stand apart from the playfulness and enable consideration of the serious and at times painful parts of life amid such joyful celebration of it.

My Hat and All That

Tony Mitton, illustrated by Sue Heap

DAVID FICKLING BOOKS (2006) PB £3.99. ISBN: 0 440 86725 8

A fabulous collection of 30 poems that celebrated poet Tony Mitton uses in performance. This book includes action rhymes, riddles and performance poetry. An especially useful section is 'At my fingertips: poems to make me move', which includes ideas for hand movements alongside the verses. This is perfect for encouraging confidence in adults who are just starting to read aloud to an audience of children, as well as increasing the enjoyment for children who can now learn 'dance steps' to accompany the poetry. The other sections of the book do not include such instructions; however, it is easy to see how the poems could lend themselves to being read aloud. For children reading the poems to themselves, the line drawings by Sue Heap keep the feel of the book light whilst stimulating. The slimness of the book and the large amounts of space on each page help to make it an undemanding introduction to poetry for children.

Omba Bolomba: Imaginative and Original Poetry for Children

Gerard Benson, illustrated by Cathy Benson

SMITH/DOORSTOP BOOKS (2005) PB £6.00 ISBN: 1 902382 70 6

This is a slim collection of original verse by Gerard Benson composed for a child audience. Ranging from nonsense verse to subjects such as night-time fears, ghosts, and riddles, Benson's poems are full of imaginative and playful language often combined with a strong element of humour and an awareness of subjects that interest children. As varied as the language, are the forms of poems. Benson makes use of traditional ballad structures, limericks, blank verse, haiku and even shaped poems among others. Nor does he assume that children are unable to make connections as he makes a nod to Edward Lear with his poem 'How pleasant to know Mr Benson' and to Carol Ann Duffy whose 'Overheard on a Salt Marsh' receives a humorous take in 'Overheard on safari'. This is a lively collection by a poet who does not rely on obvious humour and popular forms to engage the attention; it would be an excellent addition to any classroom.

Once Upon an Animal

Faustin Charles, illustrated by Jill Newton

BLOOMSBURY CHILDREN'S BOOKS (1998) PB £3.99 ISBN: 0 7475 3865 4

Charles has created a collection to satisfy nature-lovers of all ages, with poems to cover the whole animal kingdom from ants to zebras, by way of dinosaurs, platypuses and antelopes. There's also a line drawing of each creature. Charles's style incorporates fact ("Fan the flame, moth; / soft cloth / Eater of flying spark / Flutters light in the dark") as well as fantasy ("The dogs barked and joked, / Drums beat and broke / And a giant cherry-cake spoke!") and he is not afraid to tackle the less-pretty side of nature ("The nasty laughing mouth / Tearing red / Breaking bodies and / Waking the dead"). This is a great volume for educating children about the way rhymes work, as well as about the animals themselves. It also provides a good source of inspiration for those wanting to write their own nature poems.

Only One Of Me

James Berry

MACMILLAN CHILDREN'S BOOKS (2004) PB £4.99 ISBN: 0 330 41831 9

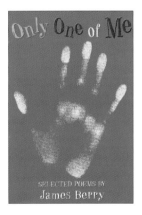

This book is a selection of nearly 100 poems from each of James Berry's four collections of poetry for children, and includes eight previously unpublished pieces. Berry believes in the importance of each person having their own culture and experience reflected in the books they read, and a theme running through this book is how children of Caribbean origin can learn to live proudly in this country. There are also poems introducing strong girls and sensitive boys, poems revelling in physical activity, poems and proverbs that celebrate Jamaican culture, as well as nature and animal poetry. The content is divided between poems in standard English, poems in Creole, and poems where the vocabulary is standard English, but whose rhythm and syntax echo the Creole language. All have a musical quality and beg to be spoken out loud. To read Berry's poetry for children is to discover our own value and uniqueness, a message insisted upon by the title poem: "I am just this one. / Nobody else makes the words / I shape with sound, when I talk". Shortlisted for the CLPE Poetry Award 2005.

Paint Me A Poem: New Poems Inspired by Art in the Tate

Grace Nichols

A & C Black (2004) hb £12.99 isbn: 0 7136 6648 x

This wonderful book is a celebration of how art and writing can influence and inspire each other. Grace Nichols was the first Writer-in-Residence at Tate Britain and she worked with children from London schools. As well as the poems written by the children, Nichols was inspired to write over 25 new poems for this collection. The paintings and sculptures were carefully chosen and as you move through the book, Nichols gives her own personal reflections under the different themes that include: animals, faces, stories in the paintings and body language. Sources of inspiration for the poems include 'The Snail' by Henri Matisse, portraits of Elizabeth I by Nicholas Hilliard and Marilyn Monroe by Andy Warhol, two Pre-Raphaelite pictures – 'Proserpine' by Dante Gabriel Rossetti, and 'Ophelia' by John Everett Millais – and the sculpture of the 'Little Dancer Aged 14' by Edgar Degas. Also included in the book is an interesting article by Colin Grigg, Head of Young People's programmes at Tate Britain and an excellent section of activities and practical ideas to help inspire children to write their own poetry.

Pants on Fire

Paul Cookson, illustrated by David Parkins

Macmillan Children's Books (2005) pb £3.99 isbn: 0 330 41798 3

This is a very enjoyable, lively modern collection. There is much silliness and word play but it also makes its points. There is the stark warning against depression in 'Beware of the Grey' and a very moving and chilling remembrance of 9/11 in 'Three-minute Silence, Three-minute Poem'. However the main theme is humour and it is very funny. There are performance poems begging to be read out loud like 'Whatevvaa…(Let's All Do the Drama Queen)' and 'Gerri the Gerbil's Workout Programme'. And there are verses that throw an amusing light on everything from our hands through our friends and family to readily recognisable situations and thoughts. Simple words work hard and to great effect for Cookson to get his punchlines and for the reader to see how many meanings a word or phrase can have. The black-and-white cartoon illustrations by David Parkins add more humour to the book and closely match the tone and meaning of the text.

Please Mrs Butler

Allan Ahlberg, illustrated by Fritz Wegner

PUFFIN BOOKS (1984) PB £4.99 ISBN: 0 14 031494 6

Please Mrs Butler

Verses by Allan Ahlberg

Since it was first published in 1983 *Please Mrs Butler* has already become a household name and a contemporary classic in its own right. This is a thoroughly enjoyable collection of school verse. The book is divided into four chapters: School Time, Play Time, Dinner Time and Home Time. Each poem is characterised by the school events and situations that most of us can relate to. 'Who Knows?' poignantly describes the stubbornness of two boys and the lack of trust they have of each other, while in 'Excuses' we can all sympathise with the pupil who is confronted by his teacher for not having done his homework and comes up with the most ridiculous excuses. The author was a teacher and has a thorough understanding of how children behave and the portrayal of how children perceive their peers and their teachers is masterfully accomplished in this volume. Fritz Wegner's illustrations are precise in detail, adding an extra dimension to each poem. A must for everyone who goes to school or for the grown-ups willing to revisit their own school memories.

The Poet Cat

Grace Nichols, illustrated by Bee Willey

BLOOMSBURY CHILDREN'S BOOKS (2001) HB £3.99 ISBN: 0 7475 5272 X

POETRY

The Poet Cat

GRACE NICHOLS

In this beautiful collection of 32 poems, Nichols has given her cat 'Thesaura' a voice that captures the very essence of a cat spirit. The poems express different viewpoints, shifting between the human views of the poet and her daughter and the feline point of view of Thesaura herself. Each poem describes a different aspect of her owner's and her own life, and they are by turns exasperated, playful and entrancing. 'Drat-the-Cat', expresses the reservations of getting a cat and there is the Poet's 'Red Alert' ("there's a cat among my poems"), the delightful 'Cat-Rap' and 'Cat-shots' and the voice of Thesaura in 'Sleeping Out' which displays a wonderful insight into her fiercely independent spirit. With sensitive black-and-white illustrations by Bee Willey, this will make an ideal gift book for any cat-lover as well as those who love poetry.

Rhyme Stew

Roald Dahl, illustrated by Quentin Blake

Puffin Books (1990) pb £4.99 isbn: 0 14 034365 2

Irresistible and outrageous as all of Roald Dahl's stories, this collection of poems will be hard to put down for adults and children alike. The appeal of the verses must lie in the tone of voice of the narrator who is always on the side of the young reader and never hesitates to put adults in their place! Some of Dahl's verse may appear to have been written with an adult audience in mind, like 'Hot and Cold' for instance where we see a woman undressing in front of a young boy. Dahl has taken well-known characters from fairy stories, nursery rhymes and fables and has adapted them to suit the taste of a more critical and sceptical contemporary audience always hungry for humour and surprises. Featured here are 'Dick Whittington and his Cat', the story of 'The Tortoise and the Hare' and how they were deceived by the cunning Rat, 'The Emperor's New Clothes', 'Ali Baba and the Forty Thieves' and 'Aladdin and his Wonderful Lamp', just to mention a few. Quentin Blake's original illustrations are the essential complement to this hilarious and enticing text.

Robocat

Adrian Henri, illustrated by Wendy Smith

Bloomsbury Children's Books (1998) pb £3.99 isbn: 0 7475 3863 8

A tiny book of poems by an iconic member of the Liverpool Scene, whose parallel career as a painter and involvement with the 1960s pop music world are both evident in the pictures he paints with such a few carefully chosen words. These are quirky pieces, some very short and apparently throwaway, but full of closely observed detail and concise description – closely echoed by the illustrations. Some are just funny – like 'Smelly'. Henri discusses gender expectations, school, haiku, poets, refugees, cats and dogs with equal attention, but it is in his landscape poems like 'The Stiperstones' that his artist's background emerges powerfully. In 'The Lion in Derbyshire' he writes about the series of paintings by George Stubbs, 'Horse Frightened by a Lion', pointing out the anomaly of a lion in Derbyshire. This could certainly encourage readers to investigate not only Henri's work in other media, but also Stubbs' work and discover that although the painter based his work on an antique Italian sculpture, he used Cresswell Crags in Derbyshire for the background. Thought-provoking poetry for all ages, excellent for reading aloud but also particularly suitable for newly confident readers.

Songs and Verse

Roald Dahl, illustrated by various artists

JONATHAN CAPE (2005) HB £14.99 ISBN: 0 224 07038 X

Songs and Verse is a sumptuous collection of some of the best of Roald Dahl's verses from his novels and stories as well as individual poems and even a few surprises with some unpublished work. With an introduction and opening illustrations to each of the seven themes by Quentin Blake, together with an assortment of twenty-five talented artists who were asked to interpret Dahl's verse — including Russell Ayto, John Lawrence, David McKee, Helen Oxenbury and Chris Wormell — the book is a visual feast, zinging with colour and wit: 'Snow-White and the Seven Dwarfs' charmingly illustrated by Babette Cole; 'Goldilocks and the Three Bears' in instantly recognisable collage style of Lauren Child; 'Goldie Pinklesweet' from *Charlie and the Great Glass Elevator* who experiences something terrible when she takes too many of her Aunt's chocolate-coloured pills, illustrated by Tony Ross; and Augustus Gloop and Mike Teavee from *Charlie and the Chocolate Factory*, delightfully illustrated by Mini Grey and Posy Simmonds respectively. This is an ideal book for any Dahl fan and one you will definitely want to keep.

Staying Out Late, Playing Out Late and Other Poems

Paul Cookson, illustrated by Nigel Baines

LION CHILDREN'S BOOKS (2003) PB £3.99 ISBN: 0 7459 4812 X

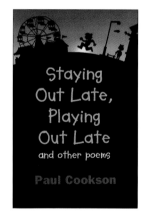

This wide-ranging collection of poems by Paul Cookson sits comfortably among poetry for young, independent readers. It contains cheerful, unapologetically silly verse about the freedom of the summer holidays, the confusion of first crushes, the mysterious ways of parents, playing games and keeping secrets. Amid the fun and the fatuous is serious, reflective verse about the abuse of children, social exclusion and knowing the difference between right and wrong. Cookson writes equally well in short rhyme and free verse and he smoothly moves between the serious and the silly without a jarring effect, perhaps because he is able to think with the mind of a child, ever wondering, never condescending or lecturing. By far the best poem in the collection is 'Love poem for . . .': "You touch all my emotions / Just me and you and a comfy chair". Children are likely to respond to these poems as if they were written especially for them by a very good friend.

Thawing Frozen Frogs

Brian Patten, illustrated by Chris Riddell

PUFFIN BOOKS (2003) PB £4.99 ISBN: 0 141 31651 9

The prolific Brian Patten presents us with yet another original poetry collection, a successful synthesis of the fantastical and the funny, the real and the reasonable. Patten writes on a wide variety of topics in both free verse and rhyme, always with an unorthodox and mischievous tone that will not fail to entertain. Explaining that 'Grown-ups are groan-ups' because 'they groan on about it,' Patten goes on to explore the strange, the disgusting, the disturbing and the ridiculous. Although the general tone of the collection is darkly playful, Patten weaves more serious themes amid the sharp wit. He includes, for example, a poem on aphasia with a brief definition at the poem's end, and a poem about a failed family Christmas. Originally published in hardback in 1990, this recent edition is improved by fabulously wicked black-and-white illustrations on every page by the award-winning illustrator Chris Riddell. For parents, educators and librarians in search of poetry books with clear 'boy appeal'.

To Catch an Elephant

Gerard Benson, illustrated by Cathy Benson

SMITH/DOORSTEP BOOKS (2002) PB £6.00 ISBN: 1 902382 40 4

Gifted poet Gerard Benson and his illustrator wife Cathy Benson have collaborated on this marvellous collection of favourite poems from two earlier collections as well as a selection of recent poems. Much of Benson's verse is inspired by the animal kingdom, real and mythical, yet despite the common subject matter of many of the poems, they are surprisingly wide in scope and unique in perspective. The collection includes 'The Scholar's Cat', a translation of a ninth-century Irish poem, "the first ever to mention the domestic cat", and a cleverly paradoxical instructive poem bearing the volume's title, 'To Catch an Elephant'. 'The Dragon and the Author', a poem about a writer who is devoured by the mythical beast of his own writing, is an example of Benson at his evocative best. Cathy Benson's black-and-white illustrations have the classic look of etchings or fine pen and ink drawings. Unfortunately the somewhat odd cover illustration does not really do justice to the quality of the illustrations within the volume, or of the poems, but it will take only an initial opening of the book to tempt any curious, or even not-so-curious, older child into trying Benson's imaginative verse.

Wicked World!

Benjamin Zephaniah, illustrated by Sarah Symonds

PUFFIN BOOKS (2000) PB £4.99 ISBN: 0 14 130683 1

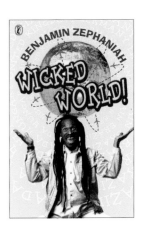

Here is a 'rapping, happening, hot and hip collection' of poems by Benjamin Zephaniah, which certainly do leap off the pages. Many of them have a solid rap beat and are themed around people and places, cultures and nationalities. Zephaniah takes the reader on a journey to Mongolia, China, Indonesia, Tibet and 'Kurdish Land' or to wander with the Roma People. Vegans, refugees and tourism are all represented here. 'Who Are We?' challenges our perception about all kinds of people and the necessity for equality. There is also the wonderful 'A Griot Writes'—a letter from 'On the streets, In Villages, Towns and Cities, Senegal, West Africa' addressed to 'Dear People' about keeping alive the oral traditions of storytelling. The poems are informative and humorous and Zephaniah is adept at getting his message across. This is an excellent collection of poetry, light-hearted yet serious and it is accompanied by striking black-and-white line drawings by Sarah Symonds.

Word Wizard

John Foster, illustrated by Ian Whadstock

OXFORD UNIVERSITY PRESS (2001) PB £4.99 ISBN: 0 19 276270 2

Word Wizard contains a variety of different poetry styles that give you a real flavour of the many ways that poetry can be written. Take the rap poem, 'The Schoolkids' Rap' or the three great 'Word Wizard' poems involving taking a word and subtracting letters until you are left with a single letter alongside a thinly shaped poem, a concrete poem – in the shape of a pneumatic drill – and some word-building poems starting with the first letter of a word, adding letters until the last line of the poem is the word itself. 'Fun With Puns', a poem about football, 'One to Eleven – Football Speak', haiku and epitaphs as well as a very moving poem about the 'Immigration Trap' all go to make this a wonderful collection of original poems in which John Foster shows that words really can be magical.

The World is Sweet

Valerie Bloom, illustrated by Debbie Lush

BLOOMSBURY CHILDREN'S BOOKS (2001) PB £3.99 ISBN: 0 7475 5115 4

In this collection of original poems, Valerie Bloom recalls everyday situations with a sense of wonder or recognition. Drawing on her Jamaican childhood as well as her English background, she presents the young reader with snapshots — tantalising narratives — describing everyday scenes and situations. From her opening image of the frost-covered world as an iced cake to the affectionate humour of 'Grandma, Bandana an' me', from the spooky 'Dem Boots' to 'The Three Ships', there is imagery to appeal to a child but with an adult message. Valerie Bloom's language is unthreatening, her images recognisable and the verse forms she chooses are traditional with a comforting sense of rhythm and rhyme. Accompanied by lively pen and ink vignettes, this is a collection that would be ideal for the classroom.

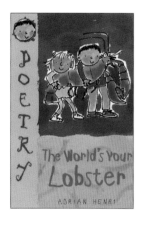

The World's Your Lobster

Adrian Henri, illustrated by Wendy Smith

BLOOMSBURY CHILDREN'S BOOKS (1998) PB £3.99 ISBN: 0 7475 3864 6

This volume brings together a collection of favourite poems from one of our best-known and most prolific poets for children. Billed as Henri's "very best", each poem is accompanied by one of Wendy Smith's charming line drawings. It's a great introduction for readers who haven't met Sammy the flying piglet or the rhinestone rhino before. It showcases the wide variety of Henri's work as he moves effortlessly between haiku, lullabies, traditional rhyming structures and free verse. His 'Conversation Between Two Cats on a Garden Wall' is a perfect example of the latter: "How are yours treating you? / Not too bad, really. / They're a bit careful with the milk". A lively way to learn how to play with words, structure verse and still be funny.

A Caribbean Dozen: Poems from Caribbean Poets

Edited by John Agard and Grace Nichols,
illustrated by Cathie Felstead

WALKER BOOKS (1994) PB £10.99 ISBN: 0 7445 5201 X

Despite the title of this anthology, there are thirteen poets included in this collection – a 'Caribbean dozen' which is explained in the introduction by the editors. With 50 poems from Jamaica, Trinidad, Guyana, the Bahamas and Barbados by well-known poets including James Berry, Valerie Bloom and Pamela Mordecai, this is a feast that captures the essence of the Caribbean; the reader is able to imagine what it is really like from the words of the people who were born there. Valerie Bloom's Jamaican rhyme 'Chicken Dinner' with a young girl pleading with her mother not to kill her chicken for dinner, "Don' cook dat chicken for dinner" or Telcine Turner's 'Charley and Miss Morley's Goat', a poem from the Bahamas together with Dionne Brand's 'River' and 'Hurricane' from Trinidad give a real flavour of the different places in the Caribbean. Each poet gives a brief insight into their childhood at the beginning of each section and full biographical details and bibliographies are provided at the end of the book. Accompanied by eighty vibrantly coloured illustrations by Cathie Felstead, this is a rich collection of poetry.

A Poem a Day

Chosen by Adrian Mitchell, illustrated by various artists

ORCHARD BOOKS (2001) HB £14.99 ISBN: 1 84121 741 7

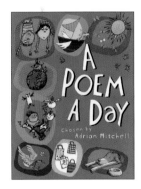

"This book was made to last" – and this is not an idle boast. Adrian Mitchell has selected a poem or part of a poem for each day of the year. In his quest he has roamed far and wide, choosing verses ranging from the traditional to the formal, from Anon to Shakespeare, Milton, Keats and on to Brian Patten, Grace Nichols and Mitchell himself via Edward Lear and Rudyard Kipling. There is no chronology and by using excerpts Mitchell encourages the element of surprise and enchantment; inspiring young readers to look for originals by whetting their appetite with a choice morsel. What fun to look up one's birthday to see what is there! Disappointed? Jump six days – or choose your lucky number. There will be something to delight every child from the gloriously sinister 'Queen Nefertiti' to the atmospheric 'Road through the Woods' or just plain nonsense. There is even a poem with no words. Not only that, there are the illustrations – lively, quirky and fun. The illustrators

capture the spirit of the anthology, making it a volume to treasure. What about that birthday present? "A poem a day helps you stop work, and play". With this collection, how true.

A Poem for Everyone

Edited by Michael Harrison and Christopher Stuart-Clark

OXFORD UNIVERSITY PRESS (2004) PB £7.99 ISBN: 0 19 276251 6

This is a gem of an anthology, containing poems about all kinds of people and including a whole host of poets, both contemporary and classic. The book starts with poems about different members of the family such as Michael Rosen's 'Mum'll be Coming Home Today' about a family's attempts to cope while mum is away, 'Mum Dad and Me' by James Berry, about the contrasts between the parents' childhood and their child growing up in the back streets of London and an amusing poem by Kit Wright ' My Dad, Your Dad', about two friends comparing their fathers. Serious poems feature here too, with 'New Baby' by Jackie Kay and 'Lies' by Carol Ann Duffy. There are poems about friendship, first love and people in general with the quirky 'Sound Collector' by Roger McGough and the very funny ' The Dirtiest Man in the World' by Shel Silverstein. Amusing black-and-white illustrations are provided by Tony Ross. This is an ideal poetry collection to dip into.

A Poke in the I:
A Collection of Concrete Poems

Selected by Paul B. Janeczko, illustrated by Chris Raschka

WALKER BOOKS (2005) PB £5.99 ISBN 0 7445 8940 1

An anthology of concrete poetry from many fine English-language poets, including John Agard, Roger McGough, John Hegley and Edwin Morgan. As the introduction tells us, "concrete poems are different from everyday poems; in fact they're a lot more playful". This anthology has many examples of the way that poems can be written to create shapes or patterns on the page that add to or actually express their meaning. The prolific and colourful illustrations are quirky, witty and gorgeous, making clever use of collage. These poems will amuse and entertain young readers. Interestingly, the gist of each one, because of the visual balance, can often be grasped at first glance, but reading the texts can present some interesting challenges; much of the writing, of course, doesn't travel simply from left to right so part of the fun is working out how to string the words together. It opens up a whole new world of possibilities for the written word and does so in artful, startling and original ways.

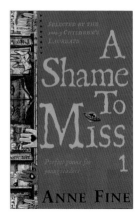

A Shame To Miss 1   A Shame To Miss 2

Selected by Anne Fine   *Selected by Anne Fine*

CORGI (2002)   CORGI (2002)

PB £5.99 ISBN: 0 552 54867 7   PB £5.99 ISBN: 0 552 54868 5

Here are two irresistible collections of poetry for young readers. Anne Fine is a life-long lover of poetry and has made a selection she feels it would be a shame for any child to miss. *A Shame To Miss 1* provides more than 70 poems with a diverse mixture of classic, well-loved poetry like Lewis Carroll's 'The Walrus and the Carpenter' or Alfred, Lord Tennyson's 'Break, Break, Break' alongside poems from more modern poets like Kit Wright with 'The Magic Box' or Brian Patten's 'Gust Becos I Cud Not Spel'. Other poets featured include Hilaire Belloc, Walter de la Mare, Eleanor Farjeon, Rudyard Kipling and many others. *A Shame To Miss 2* is the second collection that also contains a wonderful mixture of the familiar and classic from W. H. Auden, William Blake, Coleridge and Christina Rossetti to the more modern with Ted Hughes' 'Full Moon and Little Frieda', John Betjeman's 'Hunter's Trials' and Philip Larkin's 'The Trees'. There is an international flavour too, with poets from the Caribbean and China. John Agard's powerful poem 'Come from That Window Child' written in memory of Walter Rodney, a Guyanese historian and revolutionary who was assassinated in Guyana in 1980, features alongside two Chinese poets, Ping Hsin and Chang Chi. In both collections, Fine has added brief linking comments under each poem. Both these collections are ideal as an introduction to poetry.

A Spider Bought a Bicycle and Other Poems for Young Children

Chosen by Michael Rosen, illustrated by Inga Moore

KINGFISHER (2005) PB £8.99 ISBN: 0 7534 1047 8

Michael Rosen is a poet as well as a zany but very sincere advocate of the benefits of reading and children's literature. In this quirky anthology there are quite a lot of traditional playground songs and nursery rhymes by Anon, along with poems by Rosen himself, some of which

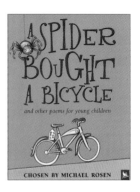

have a surprise ending that startles you into a laugh. Who knows that in 'Hey Diddle Diddle' the dish didn't run away with the spoon? In 'My Mum Said', Rosen takes words at face value with hilarious results and in 'Two Pilots' the automatic response is always wrong until you are lost for words. Alongside these are poems by Shakespeare and other well-known authors such as Tennyson, Coleridge, A. A. Milne and Eleanor Farjeon; there are verses in many moods and from different parts of the world. They all show the same love of words, rhythm and unexpectedness and are arranged in an order that adds depth and understanding to each individual poem. It is a book that, if you dip into it, gently leads you further and offers a rich experience of classic and contemporary verse. The pastel-coloured illustrations by Inga Moore reflect the poems, adding their own insight and gentle humour.

Blood and Roses: British History in Poetry

Compiled by Brian Moses

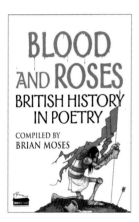

HODDER CHILDREN'S BOOKS (2005) PB £4.99 ISBN: 0 340 89388 5

This collection of 80 poems provides an exciting rhythmic journey through British history. Arranged chronologically, there is everything here from the prehistoric times to the twentieth century. These poems make history come alive and give a taste of the period – Tudor, Victorian, the Second World War – rather than just illustrating key historical events. There are excerpts from Anglo-Saxon and medieval ballads, classics from Chaucer, Rudyard Kipling, W. H. Auden and Alfred, Lord Tennyson as well as a host of contemporary poets including Charles Causley, James Berry, Judith Nicholls and Benjamin Zephaniah. The poems range from humorous to serious, covering civilizations such as the Celts and Romans as well as individual historical events like the Battle of Hastings. There are amusing poems about individual monarchs such as 'King John' by Hugh Chesterman and a tragicomic poem about 'Cardinal Wolsey' by Clare Bevan, all of which manage to convey information within some excellent rhyming verse. Illustrated throughout with black-and-white line drawings, this is an exciting way to learn about history. Shortlisted for the CLPE Poetry Award in 2005.

The Bloomsbury Book of Love Poems

Selected by Benjamin Zephaniah, illustrated by Christopher Corr

BLOOMSBURY (1999) HB £9.99 ISBN: 0 7475 4417 4

Bloomsbury has produced a beautiful collection of poems about love chosen by Benjamin Zephaniah. A whole host of poets are featured ranging from the classics with Keats and Shakespeare to the contemporary with Colin McNaughton, Brian Patten and Spike Milligan. The anguish of unrequited love is amply expressed in 'Untitled' by H. L. Brazer and the love you receive from a parent is conveyed in 'I Luv Me Mudder' by Benjamin Zephaniah. As well as featuring a 'Traditional Indian Epigram' there is a poem about disability, which explores the theme of uninhibited loving. Pat Ingoldsby's 'For Rita With Love' is both poignant and shocking: "you can't go on loving like this / Unless you are stopped / you will embrace every person you see. / Normal people don't do that". The anonymous poem, 'Children', shows how children can be affected by how they are treated – "If children live with criticism they learn to condemn" but if they learn to live with acceptance and friendship they can then learn to find love in the world. Accompanied by simplistic black-and-white line drawings by Christopher Corr, this is a unique small-format anthology to treasure, ideal to carry around and dip into.

Cock Crow: Poems about Life in the Countryside

Chosen by Michael Morpurgo and Jane Feaver, illustrated by Quentin Blake

EGMONT CHILDREN'S BOOKS (2005) HB £9.99 ISBN: 1 4052 1288 8

Young people who live in urban areas don't often get the chance to appreciate the beauty and diversity of the countryside. This poetry collection was compiled with the intention of opening eyes and hearts to the magic of the countryside. Enriched by Quentin Blake's distinctive illustrations, the verses bring home the many aspects of country living, from the variety of animals to the subtlety of the changing seasons. Beauty can be discovered in the smallest of things, even something as simple as a dewdrop swinging on a spider's thread: "Small shining drop, no lady's ring / Holds so beautiful a thing" in 'For a Dewdrop' by Eleanor Farjeon. Each poem chosen adds to the notion of nature's overwhelming vitality and builds a picture of a countryside alive with sights, sounds and smells, like the odours that rise from turned earth, rose, currant and raspberry to name but a few. Poems of Ted Hughes, D. H. Lawrence, Thomas Hardy and Robert Louis Stevenson are included, as are nursery rhymes and old country adages, making for an extremely diverse collection. Michael Morpurgo's and Jane Feaver's shared love of the countryside is evident in the verse they choose to reveal and celebrate the wonders of nature. Shortlisted for the CLPE Poetry Award 2006.

The Complete School Verse

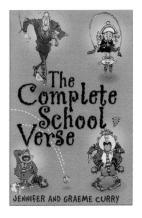

Chosen by Jennifer and Graeme Curry, illustrated by Graham Thompson

RED FOX (2001) PB £5.99 ISBN: 0 09 941754 5

Originally published as two volumes, *School Verse* and *More School Verse*, this is a collection of poems encompassing every aspect of school. The anthology includes limericks, rhymes, riddles, clapping songs all found in playgrounds around the country as well as poems and verse from well-known names such as Michael Rosen and Roger McGough. Beginning with general school poems the book is split into sections, each covering a different school theme, from starting school to home time. The reader is drawn into playground battles, served up 'Blotting Paper Pudding', given maths problems and many thoughts to ponder. Throughout the anthology small black-and-white illustrations accompany the verse and tell their own stories. The editors acknowledge the many people who helped compile the collection, including children, teachers, parents and a number of other poets, giving a wide range of perspectives and styles.

Dark as a Midnight Dream: Poetry Collection 2

Compiled by Fiona Waters, illustrated by Zara Slattery

EVANS BROTHERS (2005) HB £9.99 ISBN: 0 237 52586 0

Featuring over 250 poems, *Dark as a Midnight Dream* ranges from traditional ballads and classical verse to very modern works. Many poets will be familiar names, but some will be new discoveries. The poems cover a wide range of themes including nature and the seasons, magic and enchantment, books and poets, food, love, animals, family, war, old age and death. They explore a gamut of human emotions with plenty to inspire, amuse and move readers young and old. There are poems about going to the dentist, an African Christmas, battery hens; Alan Brownjohn's amusing 'Exploring' is about a cat taking its first tentative steps in the snow. The hauntingly beautiful 'Solitude' by Ella Wheeler Wilcox ("Laugh, and the world laughs with you, / Weep, and you weep alone") sits alongside clever poems that explore the absurdities of the English language such as 'The English Language' by Harry Hernsley or 'Have You Ever Thought' by Jacqueline Brown ("A comb has teeth but can't bite"), as well as serious poems about Aids and war. There will be something here for everyone and like all the poetry collections compiled by Fiona Waters for Evans this should be on every teacher's bookshelf.

The Forsaken Merman and Other Story Poems

Edited by Berlie Doherty, Illustrated by Nick Maland

HODDER CHILDREN'S BOOKS (2002) PB £4.99 ISBN: 0 340 68998 6

A modestly priced collection of story poems taken from a variety of sources, representing more than 200 years of verse. Doherty has made an eclectic selection that spans the tradition from ancient anonymous ballad to modern Michael Rosen, taking in Edward Lear, Longfellow and D. H. Lawrence, and many more, on the way. The selection is justified and located within the genre by a foreword in which Doherty explains the history of the story poem, and its intimate relationship with rhythm and music. As Doherty says, many of the poems in the collection are very old and have been loved by children since long ago, and it is an important aspect of the book that these can be brought to a new audience. Although some, such as 'The Owl and the Pussycat', may already be familiar to readers, this is a selection which is particularly valuable for having been made from a specific category of poetry which is often overlooked now, making it an excellent resource for teachers.

Hubble Bubble:
A Potent Brew of Magical Poems

Andrew Fusek Peters, illustrated by Melanie Williamson

HODDER CHILDREN'S BOOKS (2003) PB £4.99 ISBN: 0 7502 4119 5

A fine concoction of poems about magic, from a variety of authors from the sixteenth-century to the present, organised into six sections according to their subject and supported by title and author indexes. This is a wide-ranging anthology which will introduce readers not only to the idea that poetry can be accessible whenever it was written, but also that magic has always fascinated people of all ages. Peters has assembled seven short extracts from Shakespeare (not just the obvious Witches from *Macbeth*), as well as Keats, Coleridge, Robert Burns, Christina Rossetti, and Walter de la Mare, to compare with more recent poets' interpretations of the magical world. All the poems are given lively and amusing illustration where suitable, or a burst of magical stars and a few ingredients from a spell. Well designed, with uncrowded pages and an easily read typeface, this is a collection that will attract young readers to read for themselves and provide adults with a catholic selection of magical poems to read aloud.

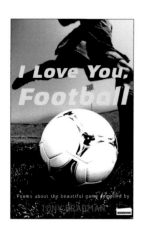

I Love You, Football

Edited by Tony Bradman, illustrated by Steve Dell

HODDER CHILDREN'S BOOKS (2004) PB £4.99 ISBN: 0 750 24279 5

This is a brilliant collection of poetry about all aspects of the beautiful game. Many well-known poets have contributed, including Jackie Kay, Allan Allberg, and Ted Hughes. The collection celebrates the diversity of the football world and all those that play, watch and enjoy it. Girls are fully included, even on active duty as in 'Girl Footballer' by Jackie Kay. The collection portrays football as a fun, enjoyable and exciting activity and is neither snobbish nor over-serious about it. There are many different styles present, including lyrical verse and ballads. There are poems in a shape and poems where the first letters of the lines form a word when read vertically, such as 'Superstition'. The illustrations are black-and-white line drawings that are varied and expressive, particularly the drawings of people enjoying the game. A great little book for any young football enthusiast.

The Kingfisher Book of Children's Poetry

Edited by Michael Rosen, illustrated by Alice Englander

Kingfisher (1998) PB £5.99 ISBN: 0 86272 784 7

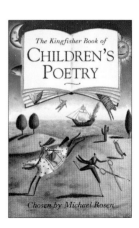

This 250 plus page selection of poetry old and new seems far more suited to an adult than to a young reader. It is an interesting selection, from Catullus to Chaucer to Charles Causley and beyond, indexed by title, first line, subject and poet, yet its rough paper, small print, crowded pages and spasmodic illustration would hardly attract an average 11-year-old. For a child already interested in poetry, however, and as a teaching resource, it has much to recommend it, as it includes such an eclectic selection of poetry. The main body of poetry is organised alphabetically by author and there are traditional or anonymous subsections of ballads, limericks, riddles and nonsense verse. It is particularly good to see excerpts from verse plays and longer poems included, and a substantial quantity of material in translation, from a variety of languages both ancient and modern. For reading out loud to a child audience, there are poems suitable for age five onwards. For young readers themselves, it is likely to interest 11 and older.

The Kingfisher Book of Scary Poems

Chosen by Gillian Clarke, illustrated by Justin Todd

Kingfisher (2003) PB £8.99 ISBN: 0753408856

First published in 1996 under the title *The Whispering Room: Haunted Poems*, this is an attractively presented collection on a popular theme. Gillian Clarke says in her introduction, "Haunting is all about imagination, and the best imaginers are poets and children". As this collection shows, some words can make your skin prickle like *wraith* or *phantom*. Some combinations of words are frightening. Some situations and places definitely call for bravery like a foggy lane on a November night. But why should a teddy bear be scary? It's all in the combination of words and imagination. We like the swooping, heart-clenching shiver of fear as long as we fall to safety at the end. That's what you can achieve with these poems. They range from traditional rhymes to works by classic and contemporary poets. There are haunting images, descriptions and stories filled with ghosts, skeletons, witches and wizards from around the world. Justin Todd's atmospheric full-colour illustrations heighten the spookiness and drama of the verse.

THE KINGFISHER POETRY LIBRARY

Haven't You Grown! Poems about Families

Selected by Belinda Hollyer, illustrated by Holly Swain

KINGFISHER (2004) PB £6.99 ISBN: 0 7534 0994 1

The Kingfisher Book of Comic Verse

Selected by Roger McGough, illustrated by Caroline Holden

KINGFISHER (2004) PB £6.99 ISBN: 0 7534 1059 1

A World of Poetry

Selected by Michael Rosen, illustrated by Larry Wilkes

KINGFISHER (2003) PB £6.99 ISBN: 1 85697 221 6

The poems in *Haven't You Grown!* reflect and explore a wide range of emotions. There is a balanced mix of humorous verse, poems that celebrate the family and others that acknowledge the pain that can be associated with it. Poems here explore the differences between generations' experiences, the pain of the loss of a loved one through death or divorce, the frustrations of being the youngest child, and the embarrassment older relatives can cause. Poets from a variety of ethnic backgrounds offer their experience of the family. Poems here involve different types of families, step-families, adoptive families, being an only child, and lone-parent families. The poems, a mix of free verse and traditional forms, arranged thematically, are clearly presented and perfectly accompanied by Holly Swain's expressive and endearing drawings.

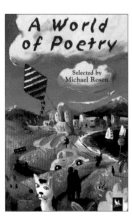

Sold together with *Haven't You Grown!* are *The Kingfisher Book of Comic Verse* and *A World of Poetry*. Arranged thematically, with illustrations by Caroline Holden, *The Kingfisher Book of Comic Verse* is a fine introduction to humorous poetry, complete with wordplay and limericks, nonsense poetry and parody, dark humour, and poems by the classic comic poets. *A World of Poetry* is one of the most diverse anthologies available. It includes ballads by Bob Dylan, Swampy Cree dream poems, translations from Old English and Old Norse, Aztec poems, as well as verse by modern poets from around the world. The poems are indexed in several different ways, giving access by form, nationality and subject. All three books in *The Kingfisher Poetry Library* are individually praiseworthy, but, while the other two books were originally published over 15 years ago, *Haven't You Grown!* stands out as being fresh and new, due to the predominance of contemporary poets and references.

Look Out! The Teachers are Coming

Chosen by Tony Bradman, illustrated by Michael Broad

MACMILLAN CHILDREN'S BOOKS (2005) PB £3.99 ISBN: 0 330 43351

An anthology of poems all about school, many by distinguished authors including Brian Moses, John Mole and Helen Dunmore. The illustrations are black and white, and provide a witty counterpoint to the poems. Because of the variety of poets included in the book, the approach and subject matter are hugely and deliciously variable. Most but not all of the poems are written from a child's perspective. For the most part this group of poems eschews the obvious; for instance Addy Farmer's 'There are Giants in my School' is an unusual take on the very young child's view of the children in Year 6, and Helen Dunmore's 'School Midnight' is a spine-tingling account of school life, time-travelling back to the nineteenth century and 'ghostly rows of whispering children'. Generally the poems in this book are sophisticated and challenging but not by any means inaccessible, often offering a new and enlightening perspective on potentially ordinary experiences. Belied by its cover illustration, this is a seriously meaty read.

Once Upon a Poem:
Favourite Poems that Tell Stories

THE CHICKEN HOUSE (2004) PB £7.99 ISBN: I 904442 74 9

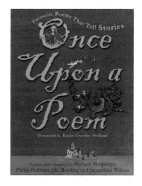

This book contains well-loved narrative poems, principally of British and American origin, such as 'The Highwayman', 'A Visit From St Nicholas' and 'Jabberwocky', as well as more contemporary pieces such as Tony Mitton's rap poem retelling the Minotaur myth and Roald Dahl's roguish rendering of the Goldilocks story. Each poem is 'championed' in a short introduction by a well-known children's author, and the book uses four different illustrators to capture the moods of the poems chosen. There is a foreword by Kevin Crossley-Holland and biographies both of the poets and of their children's writer 'champions'. The long story poems are flanked by two shorter poems, one by Roger McGough, which celebrates the narrative poem genre, and the other by Langston Hughes who beautifully reduces it to its simplest form. Every one of these poems tells an exciting story and a strong sense of rhythm and rhyme unites them all, making this book perfect for reading aloud. A wonderful idea for a book – great story-tellers introducing great story-poems – is consummately achieved by *Once Upon a Poem* and its many enthusiastic contributors.

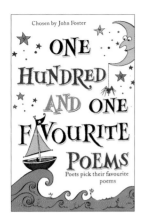

One Hundred and One Favourite Poems

Chosen by John Foster, illustrated by Clare Mackie and Tim Stevens

COLLINS (2003) PB £5.99 ISBN: 0 00 714438 54

This is an outstanding anthology compiled by John Foster of 101 poems. Each of the poets featured has been asked to choose one of their own favourite published poems. Each selection is also accompanied by a brief explanation, which gives the reason for their choice. Obviously the result is as disparate as the wide diversity of poets featured: there are poems about animals, ghosts, honey, teachers, school and much more. Poets included are Valerie Bloom, James Berry, Helen Dunmore, Gareth Owen and Paul Cookson, but there are also others who are better known for their fiction work like Malorie Blackman or Kevin Crossley-Holland. The poems are arranged in alphabetical order by the poet's surname. Each chosen poem has its own peculiarity. For instance, John Cunliffe's 'If You Come to Our House' is about a ghost that will scare readers and listeners; it's crying out to be performed in front of a group of children, while 'Horrible Henry' by Pam Gidney introduces a bully who, deservedly, is turned into a frog by a witch. Foster has been described as 'a master of anthologies' and this magnificent collection shows why. The contrasting styles of the two illustrators, Clare Mackie's funny and expressive illustrations and Tim Steven's more realistic drawings, perfectly encapsulate the spirit of the text.

Poems from Many Cultures: Poetry Collection 4

Compiled by Fiona Waters

EVANS BROTHERS (2006) HB £11.99 ISBN: 0 237 52104 0

Rainbow World: Poems from Many Cultures

Edited by Bashabi Fraser and Debjani Chatterjee,
Illustrated by Kelly Waldek

HODDER CHILDREN'S BOOKS (2004) PB £5.99 ISBM: 0 340 90318 X

Masala: Poems from India, Bangladesh, Pakistan and Sri Lanka

Chosen by Debjani Chatterjee

MACMILLAN CHILDREN'S BOOKS (2005) PB £4.99 ISBN: 0 330 41501 8

These three anthologies take the reader on a poetic journey around the world and give a real flavour of different cultures, customs and beliefs. Both *Rainbow World* and *Poems From Many Cultures* have an eclectic collection of poems from African, Asian, Caribbean and Aboriginal cultures, the latter also covering South America, Russia and Europe. *Masala* concentrates on the Indian subcontinent with poems from India, Bangladesh, Pakistan and Sri Lanka. Each book covers a variety of themes including race, cultural and national identity, family life, the environment, food, festivals, travel, mystery, myth and magic.

Poems From Many Cultures includes 95 poems that often tackle difficult subjects. From Russia comes a heart-felt poem, 'Schoolmaster', an observation by pupils of their schoolmaster as his life disintegrates around him. The short, blunt poem from Vietnam ' The Rich Eat Three Full Meals' and the startlingly brutal 'The Raid' from Italy or the haunting words of Pastor Niemöller from Germany in 1938 contrast with a descriptive poem from South Africa 'Inside my Zulu Hut'. An accompanying 'Poetry Resource Book' (ISBN: 0 23752472 4) containing photocopiable worksheets is a useful addition for teachers.

Rainbow World has over one 100 contributions from a whole host of contemporary and traditional poets that include Valerie Bloom, Grace Nichols, John Agard, Jackie Kay, Benjamin Zephaniah and Rabindranath Tagore. The content varies in form and style with a whole range of poems to choose from. The powerful poem 'Africa' from Senegal about the bitter taste of liberty and John Agard's 'Windrush Welcome', a poem of the *SS Empire Windrush* that brought 492 West Indian emigrants to Britain in 1948, contrast with a traditional Punjabi rhyme, 'The Suvan Festival' from India.

Masala includes over 140 classic and modern poems in a mixture of free and rhyming verse. Like *Rainbow World* it has similar chapter headings, but also includes story poems such as 'The Snake-Charmer's Wife' by Ian Emberson and inspirational poems like 'I Don't Know Much About India' by Nick Toczek or 'Bedeh' by Shafi Ahmed about the water-gypsies who live on boats in Bangladesh and the beautiful, lyrical 'Palm-Tree' by Rabindranath Tagore. All three anthologies give a wonderful flavour of many different cultures from all parts of the world and would be a welcome addition to any school library.

Poems Out Loud

Selected by Brian Moses

Hodder Children's Books (2004) PB £4.99 ISBN: 1 340 89401 6

"Scary, funny, joyful, sad . . . this is a collection that will delight all readers at home or in school." It includes raps, story poems and poems from other cultures. Brian Moses has brought together the works of poets such as Adisa, Debjani Chatterjee, Valerie Bloom, Wes Magee, Grace Nichols, Michael Rosen, Lewis Carroll and William Blake, to produce a vibrant collection of traditional and modern poetry for reading aloud . . . in fact, it does exactly 'what it says on the tin'! All the poems are performed by the poets on an accompanying CD. Oral poetry is a great way of introducing poetry to young people who may be shy, or even afraid, of poetry as a literary form. So, invites Moses, "Shout, sing, dance, play a drum – these are performance poems. Try them out".

Poems Then and Now: Poetry Collection 3

Compiled by Fiona Waters

Evans Brothers (2006) HB £8.99 ISBN: 0 237 52936 X

This is a school edition of an anthology first published five years ago. It is arranged thematically, with poems grouped into categories such as life cycle, natural world, war, and time. While some sections – such as that on the open road – have only two poems, others have far more, and the selection is imaginative and wide ranging. The key feature of this anthology is the juxtaposition, usually on facing pages, of old and newer poems on the same theme. This results in an emphasis on the subjects with which poets have engaged over the centuries, and the opportunity to compare the similarities and differences in their approach, their views, and their language. On each spread the older poem appears on the left, in an older italic font, while on the right, the later poem appears in a modern typeface. Throughout there is an imaginative and sensitive use of photography to highlight the theme of the section or of individual poems. This is an excellent small anthology, which includes some of the best poetry ever written, invitingly presented on good quality paper. Useful for seven upwards and older classroom teaching, this would also be an attractive introduction to fine poetry for individual readers.

Poetry Jump-Up:
A Collection of Black Poetry

Compiled by Grace Nichols, illustrated by Michael Lewis

Puffin Books (1990) pb £4.99 isbn: 0 14 034053 x

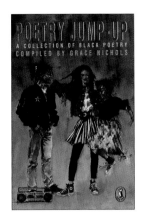

This is an anthology of poetry from around the world, divided into loose poetic subject sections with titles such as 'The Beauty of It' and 'Way Down In the Music'. The book is dotted with simple but charming black-and-white illustrations. There is also an interesting introduction by the editor Grace Nichols, who is herself a well established black British writer, setting out the arguments in favour of a book dedicating itself to 'Black Poetry'. It is an exciting collection, displaying the talents of some very well known black writers – Langston Hughes, John Agard and Benjamin Zephaniah are represented here – as well as some lesser-known poets. Overall there is a huge energy behind much of the verse – it leaps off the page, begging to be read out loud and indeed, performed. For the most part, the poems are rhythmically strong, and the use of language rooted in the sounds as well as the meanings of the words makes it easily accessible to children and a good springboard for them to start writing their own poems. An excellent and enthusing introduction to Black Poetry.

The Poetry Store: Your one-stop shop for poems!

Compiled by Paul Cookson

Hodder Children's Books (2005) pb £6.99 isbn: 0 340 89386 9

The Poetry Store is an astounding anthology of 448 pages, divided into 27 chapters, each one tackling a specific subject: brothers and sisters, mums and dads, grandparents and other relatives, school, friendship, seasons, Christmas, animals, weather, food, senses, feelings, festivals and much more. There are poems by well-known poets such as John Foster, Charles Causley, Benjamin Zephaniah, Brian Moses, Christina Rossetti, D. H. Lawrence and many others. The index of different types of poem will prove useful as it lists the wide array of poetry featured in this volume: acrostics, alliteration, alphabets, couplets, limerick, rap, sonnet, haiku and narrative just to mention a few. This book is a must for all primary school teachers looking for an appropriate poem to use on a specific subject and to support a lesson plan or assembly, but it will also prove ideal for keen poetry readers as well. Paul Cookson's 'These are the Hands' is an amusing poem to perform in front of a group of children, as there are lots of hand movements that can be imitated, while 'I Energise Your Radio' by Richard Caley is a poem about electricity written in the form of a riddle and Jill Townsend's 'Listen Here' is a poem about sound in the shape of a shell. With a poem for every occasion, this superb anthology will stimulate and delight both children and adults.

READ ME and Laugh: A Funny Poem for Every Day of the Year

Chosen by Gaby Morgan

MACMILLAN CHILDREN'S BOOKS (2005) PB £6.99 ISBN: 0 330 43557 4

A hilarious new edition to the 'Read Me' series, this anthology contains a diverse and entertaining array of funny poems for every day of the year. Chosen by Gaby Morgan, many of the rhymes befit their respective months. The collection opens with a quirky New Year resolution poem from Steve Turner. By July we are playing tennis courtesy of David Harmer and in October Gareth Owen suggests it is time to wear wellingtons again. It is awash with contributions from some of the most prestigious and popular children's poets including Roald Dahl, Spike Milligan, Brian Patten and Valerie Bloom. The form of the poems ranges from long narrative rhyme to short limerick verse and there is an appealing assortment of subjects from Chrissie Gittin's modern 'Government Health Warning' to Edward Lear's classic 'The Owl and the Pussy-cat'. Contemporary or traditional, limerick or narrative, silly or surreal, Gaby Morgan has made sure there something for everyone in this fun-packed collection.

The Secret Life of Pants and other Brilliant Poems

Selected by Roger Stevens, illustrated by Nigel Baines

A & C BLACK (2006) PB £3.99 ISBN: 0 7136 7631 0

This anthology will make you squirm and laugh out loud. Stevens has put together a very eclectic mix of poetry and rythme. Grouped under eight themed chapters these poems will make you laugh, scare you, make you thoughtful, make you sad and reveal things that you wish had been kept secret. The collection includes a wide variety of genres and styles, from haiku and limericks to sonnets, nonsense verse and sestinas. The expected selection of 'pants' poems will be appreciated by their young readers with the title poem, 'The Secret Life of Pants' by Andrew Sharick or 'The Proud Pants Parade' by Clare Bevan, but there are also poems dealing with death and bereavement ('Mum's Grave' by Roger Stevens and 'Grandad's Woollen Scarf' by Lisa Watkinson). Richard Edwards' clever parody on a song from *The Sound of Music* 'My Not Favourite Things' and the complete nonsense verse of 'A Week of Difficulties Involving Cucumbers' by John Coldwell are just some of the wonderful poems featured here. The text is accompanied by the black-and-white illustrations of Nigel Baines.

Sensational! Poems Inspired by the Five Senses

Chosen by Roger McGough, illustrated by Sara Fanelli

Macmillan Children's Books (2005) PB £4.99 ISBN: 0 330 41344 9

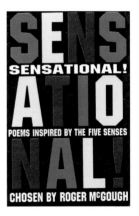

Winner of the 2005 CLPE Poetry Award, this collection of poems 'inspired by the five senses' lives up to its title in every way. It is a splendid example of the universality of good poetry, as adults are certain to appreciate the verse in this collection every bit as much as young people. Roger McGough brings together along a single theme poems by world-renowned poets, American and British, such as T. S. Eliot, William Wordsworth, Ralph Waldo Emerson, Langston Hughes, Adrian Mitchell, David Harsent, Michael Rosen and Charlotte Zolotow. McGough's fresh approach of organizing the poems according to one of the five primary senses, and beginning with poems about the senses more generally, provides a wonderful window through which the reader can reflect upon the world of sense experience as well as thinking about the themes that animate the poetic imagination. There is not a mediocre poem to be found in this volume – every poem tickles the tongue and the mind alike and beckons you to read further. The spare black-and-white illustrations by Sara Fanelli appear only every few pages, as if by surprise, lending whimsy and accessibility to the book's design yet not detracting from the reader's own imaginings. The simplicity of design allows the poems to speak for themselves, and speak they do, most powerfully. This is a beautiful collection not to be missed and very likely to inspire new generations of poets.

She's All That! Poems About Girls

Compiled by Belinda Hollyer, illustrated by Susan Hellard

KINGFISHER (2005) HB £9.99 ISBN: 0 7534 1134 2

She's All That!, shortlisted for the CLPE Poetry Award 2006, has an eye-catching, glitter-encrusted dust jacket, with brightly coloured pictures of football-playing, trainer-wearing, and nail-varnished, sandal-wearing girls' legs. These, and the other illustrations by Susan Hellard, emphasise the book's message – that being a girl is a different experience for everyone, that, as well as sugar and spice, 'today's girls add ingredients of their own choosing'. There are poems telling of the exhilaration of physical activity and of the lack of constraint on ambition that girls in our society should feel. Other poems are concerned with physical appearance, friendship, and being in love. A particularly rewarding section of this book explores girls' relationships with older women in their families and communities. The experience of girls from different cultures is represented. There are a small number of poems by early twentieth-century poets, but most of the book reflects contemporary western living, and free verse predominates, although poets also use interesting genres such as dialogue poems, list poems and skipping rhymes. The editor of this accessible and attractive book hopes all girls will find a poem that speaks directly to them.

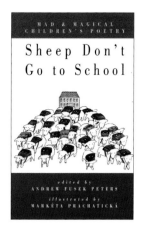

Sheep Don't Go to School

Edited by Andrew Fusek Peters, illustrated by Markéta Prachatická
Translated from Eastern European languages

BLOODAXE BOOKS (1999) PB £5.95 ISBN: 1 85224 408 9

A wonderful collection of poems from eastern Europe, representing nearly two dozen countries, and spanning cultures and generations, many translated into English for the first time, by more than forty writers who have retained the indigenous spirit of the originals. There are nursery rhymes, traditional tales in verse, riddles and new poems, all of which show the readers the similarities and differences between the stories and rhymes which exist in all human experience, and which tell us, in the most entertaining ways, about life and tradition in those countries. An excellent collection for children from eastern Europe to share with their peers in British classrooms, and a powerful tool to use in emphasising the underlying interests and concerns which affect us all. (This review first appeared in *Outside In: Children's Books in Translation*, published by Milet).z

Something Beginning with P: New Poems from Irish Poets

Edited by Seamus Cashman, illustrated by Corrina Askin and Alan Clarke

O'BRIEN PRESS (2004) HB £17.99 ISBN: 0 862789 06 0

This unusual collection of verse provides a platform for Irish literary talent. Featuring over 100 never-before-published poems from both known and lesser-known writers, it is a collection that will be appreciated not just by Hibernophiles but by anyone who likes their poetry a little off the wall. An authentic celebration of Irish talent, a number of the poems in this collection are written in Irish (but with English translations at the back of the book). A few of the poems deal with Irish themes, such as the Irish sport of Camogie in 'Straffan Camogie Girls' and a reminiscence of an Irish childhood in 'Hideout'. However, this is a varied assortment of poetry and in it you will find poems on remarkably different topics; a humorous poem about a giraffe who lived in a shoe, a haunting poem about an angel boy with unearthly powers and a heartbreaking poem about a mother parted from her child. With explosions of colour on every page the illustrations seem as much a part of the poems as the words themselves. The P in *Something Beginning with P* most definitely stands for poetry; poetry that is fun, melancholy, thoughtful, sometimes weird, but never dull. Shorlisted for the CLPE Poetry Award 2005.

The Thing That Mattered Most: Scottish Poems for Children

Edited by Julie Johnstone, The Scottish Poetry Library illustrated by Iain McIntosh

BLACK AND WHITE PUBLISHING (2006) PB £6.99 ISBN: 1 84502 095 2

It's good to see that an anthology for children of contemporary Scottish poets has been produced. This lively collection with a distinctive Scottish flavour contains poems from nearly 60 poets in English, Scots, Gaelic and Shetlandic. Each poem is accompanied by brief biographical details about the poet. There are familiar names included such as Carol Ann Duffy, Jackie Kay and Richard Edwards but there will be many that are less familiar to audiences outside Scotland. You will find a diverse mix of subjects here from the Loch Ness Monster in 'Too messy for Nessie' by Donald Nelson and 'In the Water' by Carol Ann Duffy to 'The Time Traivellers' Convention' by Sheena Blackhall where "Mary Queen o Scots arrived hersel / Signed up fur speed-datin", or 'Hiding Places' about the quiet hideaway place inside your head by Diana Hendry. With a preface by Michael Morpurgo and playful black-and-white illustrations by Iain McIntosh, this is an exciting new anthology of poetry. The book is backed up by valuable web resources designed by the Scottish Library's educational team that will prove valuable information for those studying Scottish poetry as well as being an excellent introduction to first-time readers.

Winner of the *Signal* Poetry Award

this poem doesn't rhyme

EDITED BY GERARD BENSON

This Poem Doesn't Rhyme

Edited by Gerard Benson, illustrated by Sarah-Jane Stewart

PUFFIN BOOKS (1992) PB £5.99 ISBN: 0 14034227 5

Say the word 'poetry' and 'rhyme' springs to mind but poetry is more about rhythm than rhyme. In this excellent anthology, Gerard Benson (himself a poet) has collected a wealth of great poetry that does not rhyme. His selection ranges from the Bible and traditional chants to works by Carl Sandberg, E. E. Cummings and Benson himself. The examples are imaginative and exciting; here is the possibility of real surprise as the familiar jostles with the unexpected – the mark of a good anthology. Of course, for children it is all new, and it is refreshing to have an anthology that is not afraid to introduce the young to the beauty and excitement of the past as well as the immediacy of the present. It is no surprise to learn that this anthology was awarded the Signal Poetry Award.

Why Does My Mum Always Iron a Crease in My Jeans?

Chosen by Fiona Waters

PUFFIN BOOKS (2005) PB £5.99 ISBN: 0 14 131529 6

Mike Jubb's 'Haiku', "I was daydreaming / about being popular, / and it made me smile" is just one of the many poems in this winner of the CLPE Poetry Award 2006. Fiona Waters has a knack of compiling collections which are perfect for children of all ages. The book is divided into four sections: the poems cover dealing with school, race and being different, separation and divorce, and family relationships. Peter Dixon's 'Colour of my Dreams' will resonate with many children who will understand the sentiments and be content not always to be the best at everything: 'I'm a really rotten reader / the worst in all my class . . . but none of them will ever know / the colour of my dreams". This anthology gets to the point with a collection of 'poems about important stuff' for children. Included are poems from some renowned modern poets that help a child think and ponder on life's small mysteries. How many children will linger on Lindsay MacRae's poem, 'Divorce: A Spell To Prevent It' and recognise the lines, "Perhaps it won't happen. / If I ignore it, / it won't happen. / If I try harder / it won't happen. / If I am perfect. / It won't happen"? This is an ideal book either to share and read aloud or to read in a quiet moment alone. An excellent collection of poems about 'life and stuff' which children can relate to.

Wicked Poems

Edited by Roger McGough, illustrated by Neal Layton

BLOOMSBURY (2004) PB £8-99 ISBN: 0 7475 6195 8

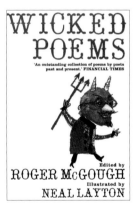

In this outrageous anthology, popular poet Roger McGough brings together a wealth of poetic talent to celebrate all that is mischievous and naughty. This is a collection where the familiar rhymes of T. S. Eliot and Rudyard Kipling battle for first place in the wicked stakes against the works of contemporary poets such as Carol Ann Duffy and Jackie Kay. The poems give voice to an array of awful characters: Shel Silverstein's selfish child who did not want to share his toys, Hilaire Belloc's infamous Matilda who could not help telling lies and McGough's very own mafia cats who are not quite what they seem. Whether mischievous or evil, these poetic creations are sure to amuse in this wickedly entertaining collection. The poems, which range from free verse to limericks, are illustrated by Neal Layton's irrepressible drawings. These conjure up the wickedness they represent with humour and skill. Funny and touching, this well chosen collection will captivate and corrupt.

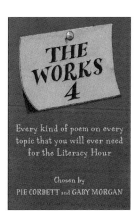

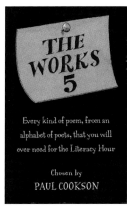

The Works 4
Chosen by Pie Corbett and Gaby Morgan
Macmillan Children's Books (2005) pb £5.99 isbn: 0 330 364 9

The Works 5
Chosen by Paul Cookson
Macmillan Children's Books (2006) pb £5.99 isbn: 0 330 39870 9

Two of a series of five books intended to supply teachers with easy accessto 'every kind of poem that you will ever need for the Literacy Hour'. These are substantial volumes which each contain several hundred poems, organised alphabetically. *Works 4* arranges poems by subject, *Works 5* by poet, and each is indexed by poet, first line and, in *Works 4*, by subject. *Works 4* also claims to include teachers' notes and a glossary of terms, including explanations of different poetic forms, and lesson ideas. While the glossary is helpful, and offers simple explanations of a variety of literary terms, the teachers' notes and the claim to lesson ideas is rather misleading, as it amounts to nine pages of very general suggestions which would be of limited use in planning a literacy lesson. *Works 5* includes no such aids, which is a pity, as the ten-page glossary from *Works 4* could usefully be included in each of the volumes. The poems in *Works 4* are mainly by very recent writers, with a handful by earlier poets included. The choice of both poems and poets is varied, with works from well-known writers such as Jackie Kay, Carol Ann Duffy, Roger McGough and Ian McMillan among less familiar or unknown names. At times, however, it appears that the editors' aim was quantity rather than quality of work.

Cookson's selection in *Works 5*, because it is poet- rather than subject-orientated, is more satisfactory, and includes greater variety, with more work from earlier poets as well as a good selection of twentieth and twenty-first century writers. Here Robert Herrick and Seamus Heaney are given equal importance, quality is not at issue, and the result is a far better balanced and more satisfying anthology. Either volume could be used selectively in the classroom from age nine onwards. While this series is primarily intended for teachers and Literacy Hour use, and there are no illustrations, the contents of *Works 5* might well appeal to older children as individual readers.

All the Things I See:
Selected Poems for Children

Jenny Joseph

MACMILLAN CHILDREN'S BOOKS (2001) PB £4.99 ISBN: 0 330 39150 X

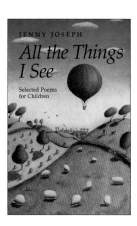

As in her widely loved 'Warning', which is included in this selection, the voices in Joseph's poems are distinctive, open and honest. The poems in *All the Things I See* sometimes deliver uncomfortable messages (notably that parents are not always patient or perceptive) and at other times joyfully celebrate her love both of particular individuals and of the natural world. While many writers for children present the child's view of adults, several of the poems here examine how adults see children – what it feels like to tidy up after them, how a parent feels when her child leaves home, and how deeply parents want to protect their children from harm. Poems in this book draw on fairy tales, classical mythology and personal memories. They range from lullabies and nursery rhymes for the youngest child to poems originally published in collections for adults. Joseph is a keen observer of animal and human life, and the world always holds interest – "Everything is news to me". She urges us in the title poem, and by example throughout this book, to make time to consider the world around us. These poems show what an enriching experience that can be.

Crash

Andrew Fusek Peters and Polly Peters

HODDER CHILDREN'S BOOKS (2005) PB £5.99 ISBN: 0 340 8846 9 X

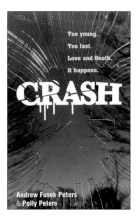

A heart-wrenching verse novel of first love and ultimate tragedy that is brought vividly to life as the story is narrated through the voices of different characters in a variety of poetic forms. Nat is the lead singer in a band and his best mate Carl plays the bass. Kate sees Nat perform one night and soon she and Nat are going out together. As their relationship develops, they fall out, make up, feel their love growing deeper and all they want to do is just be together. But in one single moment everything changes, and all the hopes and promises of the future are completely shattered. *Crash* is a deeply shocking and absorbing read, but also lyrical and funny, with the different styles of poems capturing the array of emotions associated with falling in love for the first time and the devastation of bereavement. This is a rich, thought-provoking book ideally suited for older readers.

Half-caste and Other Poems

John Agard

Hodder Children's Books (2005) PB £4.99 ISBN: 0 340 89389 3

John Agard is one of the UK's top performance poets whose English tours reach some 80,000 people each year. In this collection he explores issues of race, politics, the environment, and relationships in some of the most influential modern verse ever written specifically for teenagers. The question of race is a primary theme within this diverse compilation. In 'Checking out me History' he looks at how the black perspective on history has often been ignored. The voice with which Agard informs such issues is often as playful as it is serious as seen in his seminal work, 'Half-caste' – "Excuse me standing on one leg I'm half-caste". The poet's quirky touch is also apparent in the very format of his poetry as illustrated in 'That Mouth' which is printed in the shape of a smile. However, although his tone is often exuberant and mischievous, his writing is always probing and sincere. Extremely popular in schools, this is an important and engaging collection, which deserves to be read outside the classroom too. The depth and richness of Agard's language resonates throughout his ballads and free verse; written with humour and insight they are sure to entertain and inspire.

Hiding Out

Irene Rawnsley

Smith/Doorstop Books (1996) PB £4.95 ISBN: 1 869961 56 0

A serious collection with many of the poems about young people, and indeed adults too, on the edge of society or sometimes on the edge of danger. They don't shy away from dark and difficult areas, all part of young people's experience: running away in 'Hiding Out', the dangers of glue sniffing in 'Moody Glue' or stealing, when a child is discovered taking his father's money. They speak from many different points of view and with many different voices – the runaway, the caretaker, and the policeman for example. It is heartening to see a serious and empathic book of children's poetry, tackling some real issues without becoming didactic or simplistic and without attempting to come up with solutions. These poems are technically strong and the subject matter might well appeal to young people who wouldn't otherwise have any interest in poetry. Although some of the ideas are richly complex, the language and narrative structures are not in the least obscure, making the work very accessible. Rawnsley is well-known for her work for young people and Smith Doorstop are amongst the more well-known publishers of new poetry; this slim volume is an important addition to their list, reflecting, without compromise, a confused and complicated world.

Poems with Attitude

Andrew Fusek Peters and Polly Peters

HODDER CHILDREN'S BOOKS (2004) PB £5.99 ISBN: 0 340 90273 6

The title of this engaging collection captures the tone and mood of the poetry it contains. Separated into various sections, which include bullying and sexuality, the poems are told through a teenage voice that changes from melancholic to elated. The writers appear not to have forgotten what it feels like to be a teenager and never patronise their reader. In this diverse assortment of over 60 poems they use ballads and free verse to explore such themes as the isolation of being bullied in 'Bruises Heal' and the despair of unrequited love in 'Holiday Romance'. Although this is a serious collection, the writers have informed their poems with a quirky humour. When a mother comforts her lovelorn daughter with the famous cliché about there being plenty more fish in the sea, the daughter's response is delightfully irreverent: "Well, thank you so much for your helpful advice, / But I couldn't get off with a fish". Raw, touching and funny, this collaboration depicts the exciting and challenging world of teenagers with enthusiasm and understanding.

Sardines and Other Poems

Stephen Knight

MACMILLAN CHILDREN'S BOOKS (2004) PB £4.99 ISBN: 0 330 41356 2

You are playing sardines, and, hiding in a cupboard, wait to be found for thirty years! This collection deals with the passage of time, and with the transition between childhood and adulthood. The theme of the loss of childhood, made explicit in the poem 'Silly Me', resonates throughout the book. Poems like 'The Long Way Home', however, look forward to the autonomy that comes with leaving childhood behind. Other themes are a child's experience of conflict between parents and the loss of a father, as well as failed magicians, songbird smugglers, the disappointments of moonwalking, and the aspirations of octopus factory girls. The second section of the book is thematically linked by the poems' settings; the night, or the twilight. The reader is immersed in a world which is close yet strangely unfamiliar – life after dark. The beautifully crafted poems of *Sardines* make use of rhyme and a variety of verse forms. They speak with an intelligent understanding of what it feels like to negotiate the transition between childhood and life as a young adult. The magical yet utterly recognisable world created by Knight will illuminate readers' own experiences. *Sardines* was short-listed for the CLPE Poetry Award 2005.

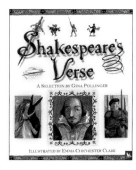

Shakespeare's Verse

Selected by Gina Pollinger, illustrated by Emma Chichester Clark

KINGFISHER (2005) PB £9.99 ISBN: 0 7534 1188 1

This illustrated anthology is an ideal introduction to Shakespeare, allowing his verse to become immediately accessible to older children. Included in the collection are 200 selected short examples of verse from Shakespeare's plays and poetry. They are arranged in thematic sections including: 'Power to Charm', 'It was a Lover and his Lass', The King is but a Man' and 'Our Revels Now are Ended'. This array of concise extracts illustrates the rich, powerful language and imagery that characterise the Bard's writing. Famous quotes from well-known plays will be recognised, but there are also lesser-known works included, as well as quotations from his poetry and sonnets. At the back of the book there is a short biography of Shakespeare, an index of plays and poetry quoted, an index of first lines and a select glossary. Illustrated by Emma Chichester Clark in her inimitable style, this is a collection to treasure.

Talking Turkeys

Benjamin Zephaniah

PUFFIN (1995) PB £4.99 ISBN: 0 14 036330 0

The king of rap poetry continues in his crusade to write poems that are fun but that also have a serious message. Zephaniah recognises that young readers and thinkers are best engaged with witty words imaginatively used, and with comical, quirky images which make several sorts of impact on the consciousness. This collection is attractively presented, using different typefaces, sizes (and orientations – as in 'Sunnyside Up') of print, and varied types of illustration, all of which grab the reader's attention visually before the intellectual message even reaches the brain. Zephaniah addresses many serious subjects: the enslaving of the African people, animals — pets, protection and persecution — while considering the place of poetry and poets in society, and casting doubt on our notions of civilization generally. Zephaniah is determined to encourage young people to write poetry themselves. This collection should certainly provide the impetus for older readers.

Two Barks

Julie O'Callaghan, illustrated by Martin Fish

BLOODAXE BOOKS (1998) PB £6.95 ISBN: 1 85224 427 5

Julie O'Callaghan's collection of poems for older children is unique. Her detailed yet accessible verse revels in the small ironies and mysteries of daily life. There is no repetition of subject matter or tone with O'Callaghan. She writes with humour and imagination about a nun on the verge of a sneeze, plants that need watering in order to bloom, the face of a girl in an old photograph, the brevity of Irish summers, or taking a break from writing a poem in order to get ice cream. The collection contains a good balance of shorter and longer narrative poems appropriate for sophisticated younger readers and challenging enough for thoughtful older readers. There is no doubt that O'Callaghan's ability to identify with her readership will put children at their ease while satisfying their craving for an most original perspective on the seemingly ordinary.

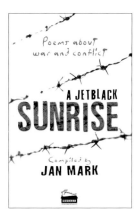

A Jetblack Sunrise: Poems About War and Conflict

Compiled by Jan Mark, illustrated by John Yates

HODDER (2004) PB £5.99 ISBN: 0 340 89379 6

A Jetblack Sunrise is a provocative and sobering anthology that has drawn on some of the greatest poems about war and conflict. Divided into four main sections: 'Peace in Our Time', 'The Dogs of War', 'Casualties' and the final chapter 'Cold and Civil' that suggests the idea – that war is the normal pursuit of mankind and peace breaks out occasionally. Most of the poems are from the twentieth century including Wilfred Owen, Siegfried Sassoon and Keith Douglas but these are placed alongside the work of contemporary writers such as James Fenton and Charles Murray as well as some classic extracts from Shakespeare and the Bible. There are many poignant poems such as 'Mort Aux Chats' by Peter Porter whichuses a metaphor to illustrate how political leadership and strong ideology can be used to indoctrinate the masses – cats are blamed for the wrongs of society while dogs are portrayed as the supreme race. 'Written in Pencil in the Sealed Railway Car' by Dan Pagis is a short poem containing a very powerful message from a desperate father (the poet himself) who was in a concentration camp during World War II. John Yates' black-and-white wood engravings perfectly accompany the glory and pathos of the text. This collection is full of raw emotion and reflects both the courage and barbarity of war.

A Shame to Miss 3

Selected by Anne Fine

CORGI (2002) PB £5.99 ISBN: 0 552 54869 3

Another superb collection of poetry selected by award-winning author Anne Fine that shouldn't be missed by any teenager. In this anthology of over 100 poems some difficult issues are dealt with. As Fine mentions in her introduction, half the adults shown this collection 'will be stabbing at the odd page muttering "This one's a bit unsuitable isn't it?"' Brian Pattern's raw poem about the consequences of what happens at a drunken party, 'Portrait of a Young Girl Raped at a Suburban Party', or the intimate poems such as Alison Prince's 'Loss' or 'The Lovesleep' by Gavin Ewart could fall into this category, but they will resonate with young teenagers. By way of contrast, Kingsley Amis' 'A Bookshop Idyll' about discovering a shelf of poetry books in a bookshop and Pablo

Neruda's beautiful poem about 'Poetry' show how important poetry is. For humour, 'Adam talks to the Press' provides a very modern interpretation of the story of the Garden of Eden by Adèle Geras. This is a collection that is ideal for older readers.

Fifty Strong: Fifty Poems Chosen by Teenagers for Teenagers

Various Editors

HEINEMANN EDUCATIONAL (2005) PB £7.25 ISBN: 0 435 30298 1

Fifty Strong is an eclectic mix of 50 poems chosen by 50 teenagers across the UK. As one would expect, a number of the poems touch on themes with which most teenagers can identify: loneliness, betrayal, love and relationships. However, this collection has not been overloaded with teen angst; wider topics such as war, imperialism, even middle age, are featured. The poems are arranged into four chapters, with accompanying notes by the teenage compilers explaining their choice of poem, what the words meant to them and how it made them feel. These notes are an interesting feature of this anthology as they provide some insight into the editing process and give a further dimension by introducing the voices of the teenagers themselves. Certain poems were included not because they were easy and enjoyable to read but rather because they were a challenge to understand. And the inclusion of a poem was not necessarily an endorsement of the sentiments expressed by the poet. For example, Spike Milligan's anti-abortion poem 'Unto Us' was included because of its thought-provoking quality even though its sentiments were rejected. The anthology features some timeless classics such as Yeats' 'He Wishes for the Cloths of Heaven' as well as some lesser-known poems. Interestingly, some of the poems are printed in their original language (including Czech, Italian and Welsh) with their English translations on the following pages. This is an inspiring and sophisticated collection chosen by teenagers for teenagers.

Selected by John Agard & Grace Nichols

From Mouth to Mouth: Oral Poems from Around the World

John Agard and Grace Nichols, illustrated by Annabel Wright

WALKER BOOKS (2004) PB £5.99 ISBN: 0 7445 8383 7

John Agard and Grace Nichols have come together to produce this enchanting collection of 'oral poems from around the world' – poems that have been passed down from generation to generation, from mouth to mouth. With beautiful watercolour and line drawings throughout, the poems are divided into nine themes including, 'On the Road', 'If you love me', 'School Time, Play Time' and 'Night Thoughts'. At the beginning of each theme the poems included in that segment are listed with their country of origin. From ocean to ocean: from Aboriginal rain chants to Dublin's Cockles and Mussels, from Gaelic Blessings to Yoroba spells to summon money, this compilation is well researched and beautifully presented. An anthology classic that readers of this age group will appreciate.

The Heinemann Book of Caribbean Poetry

Edited by Ian McDonald and Stewart Brown

HEINEMANN EDUCATION (1992) PB £0.00 ISBN: 0 435 98817 4

Here is an anthology that captures the richness and colour of the Caribbean. The editors have brought together some of the best poetry written in English in the Caribbean. There are some fine examples of poems from different parts of the Caribbean such as 'Love Letter' by Louise Bennett "(As ah puts me pen to paper / An me pen-nib start fi fly") and 'The Day My Father Died' by Mervyn Morris from Jamaica or the 'Letters From Home' by Faustin Charles and ' Trinidad if ah let yu' by Paul Keens-Douglas from Trinidad and Tobago, 'Wherever I Hang' by Grace Nichols from Guyana ("I leave me people, me land, me home") and 'Midsummer LIV' by Derek Walcott from Saint Lucia. Other well-known poets including John Agard, James Berry and Pamela Mordecai are also included. This is an ideal introduction to poetry from the Caribbean for older children.

Irish Poems

Chosen by Mathew Sweeney

MACMILLAN CHILDREN'S BOOKS

(2006) PB £4.99 ISBN: 0 330 41584 0

Scottish Poems

Chosen by John Rice

MACMILLAN CHILDREN'S BOOKS

(2006) HB £4.99 ISBN: 0 330 41584 0

Scottish Poems is an anthology for young people that includes traditional songs and the work of classic Scottish poets, as well as poems from contemporary writers. There are poems in English, Scots, Gaelic (with translations), a variety of dialects from the Highlands and the cities of the central belt, as well as a poem in the language of the Travellers. Vocabulary is explained in note form in some but not all of the poems. Notes are also included to elucidate particular historical or cultural references. John Rice, an experienced poet and anthologist, has arranged the poems thematically, so that traditional verse communes with poems by contemporary writers, and poems by Sir Walter Scott sit next to tales of disconnected phones and kitchen appliances.

Matthew Sweeney, himself the author of some wonderful books of poetry for children, writes in his introduction to *Irish Poems* that he was at first sceptical about the project because 'few of the Irish poets, today or in the past, have branched out into writing for the young'. It was the process of selecting work for the anthology that alerted him to the qualities of Irish poetry that do appeal to young people, irrespective of whether or not they are the intended audience. These are, according to Sweeney, their 'musical quality', 'narrative strength', 'metaphorical richness' and their 'sense of mystery'. These qualities are evident in this selection, which includes Irish-language poems with accompanying translations.

Although apparently similar projects, these two anthologies have quite different flavours. While *Scottish Poems* includes references to supermarkets and a contemporary, multicultural Scotland, *Irish Poems* is dominated by a more traditional and mystical feel. *Scottish Poems* includes the work of over 80 poets, while the reader can savour a more expansive selection of the work of fewer – 53 – of the Irish poets. In an attractive pocket book size, with clear type without illustrations, these two anthologies provide a rich introduction to the poetry of their respective cultures.

The Language of Love

Chosen by Anne Harvey

MACMILLAN CHILDREN'S BOOKS
(2006) PB £4.99 ISBN: 0 330 41572 7

Love

Chosen by Fiona Waters

MACMILLAN CHILDREN'S BOOKS
(2006) PB £4.99 ISBN: 0 330 48399 4

Love, a subject that will always inspire poets to put pen to paper. After all, what but love can cause so much joy and elation as well as pain and despair? These anthologies explore the various stages of love, from first love to last love, finding love to losing love, ephemeral love to enduring love. Each poet voices their attitude towards love; some regard being in love as a glorious state, others as mere folly. Losing love can be met with aching grief or with humorous disregard. So whether you believe in love or are just plain cynical about the whole thing you are bound to find verse that speaks to you. Traditionalist tastes will be satisfied by contributions from Shakespeare, Wordsworth and Yeats, with more quirky poems coming from Brian Patten and Ogden Nash. From Wales to Ancient India, these poems have been gathered from across continents and the ages. These anthologies are perfect for those romantics who just can't live without love and who want to immerse themselves in love's many changing moods. "Love comes quietly, / finally, drops / about me, on me, / in the old ways. / What did I know / thinking myself / able to go / alone all the way." (from 'Love Comes Quietly' by Robert Creeley).

Love, Hate and My Best Mate: Poems about Love and Relationships

Compiled by Andrew Fusek Peters and Polly Peters

HODDER CHILDREN'S BOOKS (2005) PB £5.99 ISBN: 0 340 89387 7

This unusual collection explores the turbulent world of love and relationships from a first date, first kiss, fighting and splitting up, to finding and losing best friends. There are lyrical pieces, email epics, text message sonnets and sad poems juxtaposed with humour under the three main sections of 'Love', 'Hate' and 'My Best Mate'. It combines both classic and contemporary works, ranging from 'It's Out At Last' by Sulpicia, a fifteen year old Roman poetess, an Anglo-Saxon poem, 'The Wife's Lament', an extract from the beautiful and moving 'Love Kept Secret' by Dafydd ap Gwilym, a 14th century Welsh poet and the translated work of Jaroslav Vrchlicky 'For A Little Love' *(from Windows in a Storm)* to the more contemporary style of Polly Peter's 'The Long Waiting'. These are in sharp contrast to Brian Patten's very funny 'His

First Love' in which he says that "Falling in love was like falling down the stairs" or Roger Stevens' parody of the poem, 'My Luve is Like A Red, Red Rose' by Robert Burns. This mixture of sad, amusing and angry poems goes to make up a unique anthology.

The Orchard Book of Poems

Chosen by Adrian Mitchell, illustrated by Chloe Cheese

ORCHARD BOOKS (1993) PB £9.99 ISBN: 1 86039 268 7

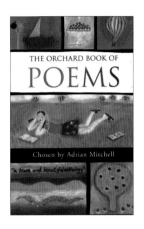

Adrian Mitchell reminds us in his introduction that long before writing was ever invented poems were being made up and shared. But somewhere along the way poetry got left behind and today many of us live without it. *The Orchard Book of Poems* aims to rekindle a love of poetry. As Mitchell says "Pick a poem, any poem, and read it to yourself, If you like it . . . it'll stay in your heart and you can use that poem whenever you need it." There are over 150 poems to choose from in this anthology which is divided into seven broad themes covering a variety of genres. Along with some of the well-known classics from Keats, Shakespeare, William Blake and contemporary poets like James Berry and Roger McGough, there are some surprises; the nineteenth-century 'The Enchanted Mistress' and 'Donall Oge' by Irish dramatist Isabella Augusta, Lady Gregory to the contemporary lyrics of John Lennon and Bob Dylan, Roger Miller's pop-song 1964, 'King of the Road'. Also featured are 'How Much Longer?' by American poet, Robert Mezey about the horrors of war and the stunning 'Sensitive, Seldom and Sad' by Mervyn Peake. This is a perfect collection in which to find, as Mitchell suggests, a poem that stays in your heart.

Out of Order: Between-age Poems

Compiled by Andrew Fusek Peters, illustrated by Clive Goodyer

EVANS BROTHERS (2002) PB £8.99 ISBN: 0 237 52316 7

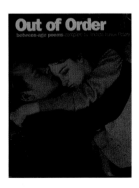

An anthology aimed at 'between-age' readers, which tries to reach out to those who are not already enthused by the genre. The underlying purpose of this selection is to prove that poetry is not difficult or irrelevant, but can deal with all the difficult situations in life – school, bullying, families, love and drugs, and that it has something funny, serious or even shocking to say about them which will make us think and may even help us in our relationships. Peters' selection is largely from modern poets, although earlier writers feature among the section on love, and includes deeply thoughtful material, such as Polly Peters' 'Kid Story / Mr Peters' which relates the same incident from two very different points of view, and considers the devastating effect of student bullying. There are some tough topics here, Seamus Heaney's 'Mid-term Break' and some of the poems about race and belonging bringing us face to face with the stark realities of prejudice, death and the minefield of teenage life. An extremely worthwhile addition to teenage reading, with Clive Goodyer's illustrations finely tuned to both subject and audience.

Overheard on a Saltmarsh: Poets' Favourite Poems

Edited by Carol Ann Duffy

Macmillan Children's Books (2004) PB £4.99 ISBN: 0 330 39711 7

In this collection each poet has not only contributed a poem but also chosen his or her favourite children's poem by someone else. They are placed next to each other so that the reader can compare and contrast the poet's work with that which they most admire. In some cases you can really see how it has influenced them, but in others you wonder what possessed them to make their selection. Jackie Kay, for example, has chosen 'Willie's Wife' by Robert Burns. In 'The World of Trees' you can see the connection between Burns's lyrical, beautiful flowing poems and Kay's own. Wendy Cope on the other hand shares little with Kit Wright, whose poem she chose. Edited by the excellent Carol Ann Duffy, who is fast becoming Britain's most read poet, this anthology makes for fascinating reading. It is amazing to get such rare insight into the minds of poets.

Poems of Childhood

Chosen by Brian Moses

Macmillan Children's Books (2005) PB £4.99 ISBN: 0 330 41567 0

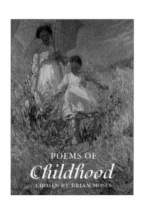

The small size of the book itself and the elegant, classic cover reproduction of Dorothea Sharp's painting 'A Morning Stroll' make it more appropriate as a gift selection for a fanciful young person or a nostalgic adult than as a stock choice for a library or classroom. However Moses, himself a respected poet for adults and children, has chosen a selection of evocative poems of childhood experience by some of the best contemporary poets writing in the English language. Moses' division of the poems into sections with titles taken from lines in the poems themselves may seem an almost random organizational method and indeed may puzzle some readers, or it might just as likely provoke them to read further to try to identify the poem to which the line belongs. This is a fine collection with perhaps a smaller possible readership than some books for young people due to its size and design but it is none the less worthy of attention.

The Poet's House

Chosen by Jude Brigley, illustrated by Fran Evans

PONT BOOKS (2001) PB £5.50 ISBN: 1 85902 602 8

An anthology of poetry from Wales that takes the reader on an illustrated, poetic journey through the rooms of the Poet's House. This selection of 77 poems by over 50 poets covers a wide range of themes. Although it is mainly a contemporary collection there are some classics and some translations from Welsh. Gerard Manley Hopkins' 'Pied Beauty' and an extract from *Under Milk Wood* by Dylan Thomas sit alongside a moving poem by Menna Elfyn, 'A Load of Coal', in memory of the poet's grandfather who was killed in the mines. The collection explores every sort of mood; the two masterly poems by Catherine Fisher, 'Words' and 'Pencils', contrast with the amusing poem of John Bilsborough, 'Back to School', about getting the teacher back to school on time and 'I'm in Love with the Girl at Tesco's Check-out Till' by Sean Dudson. The book is illustrated with pen-and-ink illustrations by Fran Evans.

Thoughts Like an Ocean

Chosen by Neil Nuttall and Andy Hawkins,
linocut illustrations by Jenny Fells

PONT BOOKS (2001) PB £5.95 ISBN: 1 85902 449 1

This is an anthology not just of poems, but more specifically, contemporary poems and more than that, modern Welsh poems by names perhaps less well known than many other contemporary poets Their subjects are drawn from everyday life – bullies, conkers, the new school; or from the family – Auntie May, baby brother, Uncle Eddie. Many draw on the Welsh landscape – particular places and particular people, the Welsh names lending a particular resonance and musicality to the lines. Some poets stand out – Huw Jones is one, while 'Y ddraich goch' by Henry Treece epitomises the imaginative background to this collection. This is an anthology that could well be used with poems drawn from other cultures to illustrate how poetry is not an expression of generalities but has its roots in real feelings of identity, real contexts.

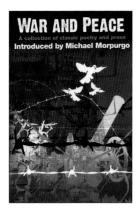

War and Peace: A Collection of Classic Poetry and Prose

Edited by Kate Agnew, introduction by Michael Morpurgo

Wizard Books (2004)

PB £5.99 ISBN: 1 84046 570 0

Life and Death: A Collection of Classic Poetry and Prose

Edited by Kate Agnew, introduction by Philip Pullman

Wizard Books (2004)

PB £5.99 ISBN: 1 84046 567 0

Fear and Trembling: A Collection of Classic Poetry and Prose

Edited by Kate Agnew, introduction by Kevin Crossley-Holland

Wizard Books (2004)

PB £5.99 ISBN: 1 84046 526 3

Love and Longing: A Collection of Classic Poetry and Prose

Edited by Kate Agnew, introduction by Jacqueline Wilson

Wizard Books (2004)

PB £5.99 ISBN: 1 84046 523 9

These four anthologies edited by Kate Agnew tackle major themes with introductions by four distinguished children's writers. *War and Peace* describes the horror and tragedy of war, the glory and the misery, set against the calm tranquillity of peace. Divided into six sections, 'Friends and Enemies', 'Leaders and Leadership', 'Wartime', 'Death and Glory', 'Remembrance' and 'Peace', the range of poetry and prose is eclectic. There are extracts from Virgil's *Aeneid* and Shakepeare's *Othello*, 'Agincourt' by Michael Drayton or a poem on the Crimea, 'The Lesson of War' by Adelaide Ann Proctor. The First World War features prominently with the works of Rupert Brooke, Wilfred Owen and the evocative 'In Flanders Field' by John McCrae. Thomas Hardy's 'Christmas 1924' is still disturbingly relevant today: "Peace on earth! was said. We sing it, / And pay a million priests to bring it. / After two thousand years of mass / We've got as far as poison-gas".

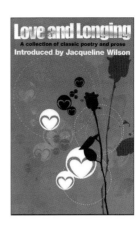

Life and Death covers the seven ages of man, a subject that has produced some of the greatest literature. Milton, Shakespeare, Tennyson, Gerald Manley Hopkins, Wordsworth, Keats, D. H. Lawrence and Christina Rossetti are just a few of the poets included. *Fear and Trembling* deals with death and the supernatural, ranging from Christopher Marlow's *Doctor Faustus* to Mary Wollstonecraft's *Frankenstein*, while *Love and Longing* espouses all the pleasures and pains of love and includes 'Sonnet 43' by Elizabeth Barratt Browning, ' La Belle Dame Sans Merci' by Keats and the poignant 'The Ballad of Reading Gaol' by Oscar Wilde. The lesser-known works of Charlotte Mew, 'I So Liked Spring' and Aphra Behn's 'Love in Fantastic Triumph State' are also featured. All four anthologies includes both poetry and prose with extracts from many well-known classics. They are ideal for older readers providing them with an ample choice of some of the best literature.

Anthology   **ALL AGES**

The Hutchinson Treasury of Children's Poetry

Edited by Alison Sage, illustrated by various artists

HUTCHINSON CHILDREN'S BOOKS (1998) HB £19.95 ISBN: 0 09 176748 2

This is a stunning collection comprising the best in contemporary and classic poetry for children. Divided into four sections – 'Nursery Rhymes and First Poems', Rhymes and Poems for the Young', 'Poems for Older Children' and 'Older Poems and Classic Poetry', it is a book designed to grow with your child. It includes the work of poets such as Michael Rosen, Roald Dahl, Brian Patten and Colin McNaughton as well as selections from Shakespeare, Robert Frost, Lewis Carroll and many more. Lavishly illustrated throughout, it features especially commissioned artwork from some of the world's finest children's illustrators – Quentin Blake, Angela Barrett, Satoshi Kitamura and Tony Ross – as well as reproductions of the work of classic illustrators including Arthur Rackham and Kate Greenaway. Here you will find Margaret Mahy's tale 'The Remarkable Cake' that was decorated by a witch, T. S. Eliot's wonderful 'Macavity: the Mystery Cat' and 'Night Mail' by W. H. Auden. In the final section there are well-known classics including Wordsworth's 'Daffodils' and the tale of 'The Pied Piper of Hamlin' by Robert Browning. This is an unforgettable treasury of over 300 of the best-loved poems and will take children on a unique journey exploring the wonders of rhyme and verse.

MANDY COE is an award-winning poet who writes for adults and children. Her poetry has been broadcast on BBC television and radio and she received a Hawthornden Fellowship in 2005. Mandy has facilitated workshops and INSET in schools and venues such as the Tate, the Barbican and the Royal Festival Hall. She works for the Children's Poetry Bookshelf, Writing Together and the Poetry Society. Her latest collection is *The Weight of Cows*, Shoestring Press. Her latest book, co-written with Jean Sprackland, is a guide to organising writers' visits to schools - *Our Thoughts are Bees: A Handbook for Writers in Schools.*

JOHN FOSTER is one of the country's leading anthologists of children's poetry. His collections range from popular books of first verses for the very young, such as *Twinkle Twinkle Chocolate Bar*, to zany collections on all sorts of topics, to wordplay, riddle and shape poems. He has collaborated with award-winning artist Korky Paul on seven books, including books of dinosaur, dragon and monsters poems and has written 11 books of his own poetry and two rhyming dictionaries. He is a well-known performance poet who has performed at football clubs and in supermarkets, as well as in hundreds of schools and libraries. A selection of three hundred of his own poems, *The Poetry Chest*, is to be published in 2007.

GABY MORGAN fell in love with Wilfred Owen at the age of 16 and discovered a whole world of poets and poetry and she has since paused to admire poets including Rimbaud, Brian Patten, Carol Ann Duffy, Wendy Cope and Billy Collins. Gaby has a French degree from UCL and has worked at Macmillan Children's Books since she graduated in 1993. She has been Editorial Director for poetry and non-fiction since 2000.

JANETTA OTTER-BARRY has worked at Frances Lincoln as Editorial Director of children's books since 1988. Janetta has a special interest in multicultural publishing and Frances Lincoln are the publishers of modern classics *Amazing Grace* and *A is for Africa*, as well as Rosemary Sutcliff's *Black Ships Before Troy.*

MICHAEL ROSEN writes 'stuff'. He doesn't mind whether it's called poetry or not, but he likes writing that sort of thing and children like reading it. Michael's parents were both teachers, and so were many of their friends. In fact, Michael claims that he believed that when he was young everyone was a teacher and, if they weren't, they ought to be! Despite this, Michael never became a teacher himself. Originally, he wanted to be an actor but then he started training as a doctor. Later on he changed to studying English at University and finally became a writer. His first collection of poems, *Mind Your Own Business*, was published in 1974. It is a collection of poems about when Michael was a boy: his relationships with his brother and his parents, and his perceptions of the world around him.

Since then, Michael has written many anthologies of poems and edited collections of classic poems. He has also written some picture books. Michael writes anywhere, scribbling down his 'stuff' on buses, trains, beaches, as well as in his own back garden.

MORAG STYLES is a Senior Lecturer at the University of Cambridge's Faculty of Education and she teaches on undergraduate, postgraduate, INSET and higher degree courses. Prior to this she was Language Co-ordinator at Homerton College for many years. Morag has written and lectured widely on children's literature, poetry and literacy. She has organised many national and international children's literature conferences and two major exhibitions at the Fitzwilliam Museum. She has just completed a research project (Reading Pictures) and is currently working in two areas: poetry for children and domestic literacy in the first half of the eighteenth century. Morag has produced several publications, the most recent of which are *Children Reading Pictures: Interpreting Visual Texts* (with E. Arizpe) (2002) Routledge and *Art, Narrative & Childhood* (ed. with Eve Bearne) (2002) Trentham Books.

RACHEL ANSCOMBE has a history degree and followed this with a post-graduate course in librarianship. She has been working with children and books in public libraries ever since, strangely only in authorities beginning with B – Bath, Bradford and now Bromley.

BRIDGET CARRINGTON was formerly a librarian and teacher and is now a reviewer and writer, with an MA in Children's Literature from the University of Roehampton. Currently undertaking a doctorate there, researching the early history of fiction for young adults.

JEMMA COOK gained a degree at King's College London and has worked in children's libraries. Jemma now works in the children's department at Ottakars Bookshop in Clapham Junction, London.

FERELITH HORDON has been a librarian for 35 years, 33 of those as a qualified Children's Librarian starting as a trainee with Hertfordshire Libraries before moving to Wandsworth Libraries in London where she has been ever since. She is currently Chair of the Youth Library Group in London.

SHELLEY JACOBSEN has a B.A. in Russian language and cultural history from Hampshire College in Amherst, Mass., an M.A. in Slavic languages and literatures from Yale University, an M.A.R. in religion and the arts from Yale Divinity School and finally an M.L.I.S. in library and information studies from University College London. Shelley now works as a children's librarian for Hounslow Libraries.

REBECCA JONES is a children's librarian for Wandsworth Libraries and was previously a librarian in Leeds.

PAULA O'CONNOR currently works as a Children's Librarian. She previously worked as a primary and nursery teacher for five years before leaving to follow her dream of becoming a children's author. She is now working on her first book and would love to see it on the library shelves some day.

ERIF PIETCH has travelled the world, working as a bookseller along the way. Currently she is working as a Children's Bookseller in Ottakars Bookshop, Clapham Junction in London.

JACQUELINE SAPHRA's plays have been widely performed in repertory theatres and on national tours. Her poetry has been published in magazines and anthologies. She received first prize in the London Art Poetry competition judged by Andrew Motion.

ANNA SMALL has a degree in Social Science. She has worked in the book industry since leaving university. Anna presently works as a senior bookseller in Ottakars Bookshop in Clapham Junction, London. There she runs a number of areas including adults' poetry.

NICOLA SMYTH was Deputy Literary Editor of the Independent on Sunday for six years. She previously worked for Oxford University Press, the Poetry Society and Arts Council England. She now works as a freelance journalist.

MANDY SOUTHERN has a history degree from Goldsmith's College and has worked with children's books since she was 18 in libraries and schools. She currently holds the position of Children's floor manager at Ottakars Bookshop in Clapham Junction, London.

MIRIAM VALENCIA is Assistant Librarian at the Poetry Library, where she is responsible for the children's collection.

EDITORS

DEBORAH HALLFORD is a freelance project consultant specialising in children's literature and arts projects. She previously co-edited *Outside In: Children's Books in Translation* (2005) published by Milet and *Folk and Fairy Tales: A Book Guide* (2004) with Edgardo Zaghini. Deborah has an M.A. in History and is a Committee member of IBBY UK (International Board on Books for Young People).

EDGARDO ZAGHINI is a specialist in children's literature having previously co-edited *Outside In: Children's Books in Translation* and *Folk and Fairy Tales.* Edgardo has an M.A. in Children's Literature, is a chartered librarian and author of *Pop-Ups: A Guide to Novelty Books* and *The Children's Book Handbook.* He has been a Committee member of IBBY, and the Children's Books History Society and is a member of the Youth Library Group.

(PBS) has a long history of supporting the sale of poetry books. Founded by T. S. Eliot and friends in 1953, it has stayed true to its original mission over the years and its core activity is little changed.

A major part of PBS's remit is to encourage young people to read and enjoy poetry. Unless children appreciate poetry from an early age, they are unlikely to read it as adults. The organisation relaunched its Children's Poetry Bookshelf (CPB) in 2005. As well as offering the best new titles, it also provides a selection of back-list titles. Its new membership schemes offer libraries a selected range of children's poetry. Parents, grandparents and other adults can give a gift membership which will deliver the gift of poetry to the child throughout the year. The educational membership has a special focus, and teachers' worksheets are freely available to all members.

The books are chosen by a panel of three expert Selectors. Fiona Waters is widely admired in the children's book world for her vast knowledge of poetry and of children's reading tastes. A former children's bookseller and publisher, she is currently the Editorial Director of Troubadour, The Travelling Book Company, and has edited 34 children's poetry collections and written 50 other books.

Wes Magee is a former teacher and a well-known children's poet who has written over 70 books. He takes his lively Poetry Show to 50 or 60 schools every year, where he entertains large numbers of children with his strongly rhythmic and child-centred

poetry. His most recent books are *The Boneyard Rap* and *The Very Best of Wes Magee.*

Mandy Coe has published two poetry collections for adults and poems for children which have appeared in anthologies. She is the author, with Jean Sprackland, of *Our Thoughts are Bees: Writers Working with Schools.* As well as being a Selector, Mandy is also the CPB's educational expert and writes the worksheets which are sent to teachers.

The CPB's new website, *www.childrenspoetrybookshelf.co.uk* has a lively children's site offering poetry quizzes and poem puzzles, as well as an adult section focusing on issues relating to children's poetry and providing assistance for teachers. All the children's poetry books in print in the UK are available online, and members can get their special discount through the members' site.

To tie in with National Poetry Day 2006, CPB will launch its first national children's poetry competition. There will be two sections, for 7 to 8-year-olds and 9 to11-year-olds. Teachers will be asked to encourage the children to write poems, which can be sent in as class entries. Individual children will be able to enter their own poems on the website.

For the Poetry Book Society itself, publishers are invited to submit their new single-author poetry collections and the Selectors choose the best book of the quarter to be the PBS Choice. They also choose four other Recommendations, a Recommended Translation and a Pamphlet Choice, which focuses

on new and sometimes self-published work.

Just as in Eliot's day, or when Philip Larkin was Chair of the Society, the PBS today has a loyal membership which is highly knowledgeable about poetry. The organisation keeps members up to date with new poetry books. The *Bulletin*, which includes pieces by the Selectors as well as contributions from the poets themselves, acts as a review of the new titles. It is also an illuminating read in its own right. The PBS is in close touch with poetry publishers and can use its expertise to track down specific poetry titles, which members can buy at a special discount.

The PBS is funded by Arts Council England and its remit is to support the sales and readership of poetry. To that end, it has developed a number of other activities directed at adults and children. In 2004 it organised the Next Generation Poets promotion, which found the most exhilarating 20 new poets of the previous ten years and organised 22 events around the UK.

Also in 2004, the PBS launched *www.poetrybookshoponline.com* a niche online poetry bookselling site which uses a data link to make available all the poetry titles in print in the UK. There are ambitious plans to develop the PBO into a poetry portal. The emphasis will be on serving readers and making poetry as widely available as possible.

Books will always be the main focus on the site, but the PBO is already moving into offering CDs and will shortly list poetry magazines as well. In 2005, it became the sole selling agent for the newly launched Poetry Archive CDs. This ambitious scheme aims to record living poets for posterity. Currently around ninety new sixty-minute digital recordings are available on CD, online from the PBO and direct from the Poetry Book Society.

The Poetry Book Society
Fourth Floor
2 Tavistock Place
London WC1H 9RA
Tel: 020 7833 9247
Fax: 020 7833 5990
info@poetrybooks.co.uk
www.poetrybooks.co.uk

Belitha Press
(Chrysalis Children's Books/Anova Books)
151 Freston Road
London W10 3HB
Tel: 020 7314 1400
Fax: 020 7314 1594
www.anovabooks.com

A & C Black
38 Soho Square
London W1D 3HB
Tel: 020 7758 0200
Fax: 020 7758 0222
www.acblack.com

Black and White Publishing
99 Giles Street
Leith
Edinburgh EN6 6BZ
Tel: 0131 625 4500
Fax: 0131 625 4501
www.blackandwhitepublishing.com

Bloodaxe Books
Highgreen
Tarset
Northumberland NE48 1RP
Tel: 01434 240500
Fax: 01434 240505
www.bloodaxebooks.com

Bloomsbury Children's Books
36 Soho Square
London W1D 3QY
Tel: 020 7494 2111
Fax: 020 7434 0151
www.bloomsbury.com

Marion Boyars Publishers
24 Lacy Road
London SW15 1NL
Tel: 020 8788 9522
Fax: 020 8789 8122
www.marionboyars.co.uk

**Jonathan Cape
Children's Books**
(see Random House)

The Chicken House
2 Palmer Street
Frome
Somerset BA11 1DS
Tel: 01373 454488
Fax: 01373 454499
www.doublecluck.com

Chronicle Books
(Distributed by Ragged Bears)

Corgi
(see Random House)

Egmont Children's Books
239 Kensington High Street
London W8 6SA
Tel: 020 7761 3500
Fax: 020 7761 3510
www.egmont.co.uk

Evans Brothers
2A Portman Mansions
Chiltern Street
London W1V 6NR
Tel: 020 7487 0920
Fax: 020 7487 0921
www.evansbooks.co.uk

Faber and Faber
3 Queen Square
London WC1N 3AU
Tel: 020 7465 0045
Fax: 020 7465 0034
www.faber.co.uk

David Fickling Books
31 Beaumont Street
Oxford OX1 2PN
Tel: 01865 339000
Fax: 01865 339009
www.davidficklingbooks.co.uk

**HarperCollins
Children's Books**
77/85 Fulham Palace Road
London W6 8JB
Tel: 020 8741 7070
Fax: 020 8307 4440
www.harpercollins.co.uk

Heinemann Educational
(Harcourt Education)
Halley Court
Jordan Hill
Oxford OX2 8EJ
Tel: 01865 310533
Fax: 01865 314641
www.heinemann.co.uk

Hodder Children's Books
(Hachette Children's Books)
338 Euston Road
London NW1 3BH
Tel: 020 7873 6000
Fax: 020 7873 6024
www.hodderheadline.co.uk

Hutchinson
(see Random House)

Kingfisher Publications
New Penderel House
283-288 High Holborn
London WC1V 7HZ
Tel: 020 7903 9999
Fax 020 7242 4979
www.kingfisher.com

KPk Books
(Distributed by Ragged Bears)

Frances Lincoln
4 Torriano Mews
Torriano Avenue
London NW5 2RZ
Tel: 020 7284 4009
Fax: 020 7485 0490
www.frances-lincoln.com

Lion Children's Books
(Lion Hudson)
Mayfield House
256 Banbury Road
Oxford OX2 7DH
Tel: 01865 302750
Fax: 01865 302757
www.lionhudson.com

Macmillan Children's Books
20 New Wharf Road
London N1 9RR
Tel: 020 7014 6000
Fax: 020 7014 6001
www.panmacmillan.com

Mercat Press
10 Coates Crescent
Edinburgh EH3 7AL
Tel: 0311 225 5324
Fax: 0131 226 6632
www.mercatpress.com

Milet Publishing
333 North Michigan Avenue
Suite 530
Chicago, IL 60601 USA
Tel: 1 312 920 1828
Fax: 1 312 920 1829
www.milet.com

Jane Nissen Books
Swan House
Chiswick Mall
London W4 2PS
Tel: 020 8994 8203
Fax: 020 8742 8198

The O'Brien Press
20 Victoria Road
Rathgar
Dublin 6
Republic of Ireland
Tel: 01 492 3333
Fax: 01 492 2777
www.obrien.ie

Orchard Books
(Hachette Children's Books)
338 Euston Road
London NW1 3BH
Tel: 020 7873 6000
Fax: 020 7873 6225
www.wattspub.co.uk

Oxford University Press
Great Clarendon Street
Oxford OX2 6DP
Tel: 01865 556767
Fax: 01865 556646
www.oup.com

Pont Books
(Gomer Press)
Llandysul Enterprise Park
Llandysul
Ceredigion SA44 4JL
Tel: 01559 363090
www.gomer.co.uk

Puffin Books
(Penguin Group)
80 The Strand
London WC2R 0RL
Tel: 020 7010 3000
Fax: 020 7010 6060
www.puffin.co.uk

Random House
Children's Books
(Random House Group)
61-63 Uxbridge Road
London W5 5SA
Tel: 020 8231 6800
Fax: 020 8231 6767
www.kidsatrandomhouse.co.uk

Red Fox
(see Random House)

Scholastic Children's Books
Euston House
24 Eversholt Street
London NW1 1DB
Tel: 020 7756 7756
www.scholastic.co.uk

Smith/Doorstop Books
The Poetry Business, The Studio
Byram Arcade, Westgate
Huddersfield
Yorkshire HD1 1ND
Tel: 01484 434840
Fax: 01484 426566
www.poetrybusiness.co.uk

Sort of Books
PO Box 18678
London NW3 2FL
(Distributed by Penguin Group)
www.sortof.co.uk

Summersdale Publishing
46 West Street
Chichester
West Sussex PO19 1RP
Tel: 01243 771107
Fax: 01243 786300
www.summersdale.com

Tara Publications
(Distributed by Turnaround
Publisher Service)

The Templar Company
Pippbrook Mill
London Road
Dorking
Surrey RH4 1JE
Tel: 01306 876361
Fax: 01306 889097
www.templarco.co.uk

Virgin Books
Thames Wharf Studios
Rainville Road
London W6 9HA
Tel: 020 7386 3300
Fax: 020 7386 3360
www.virgin.com/books

Walker Books
87 Vauxhall Walk
London SE11 5HJ
Tel: 020 7793 0909
Fax: 020 7587 1123
www.walkerbooks.co.uk

WingedChariot Press
7 Court Road
Tunbridge Wells
Kent TN4 8HT
Tel: 0779 1273374
www.wingedchariot.com

Wizard Books
(Icon Books)
The Old Dairy
Brook Road
Thriplow
Cambridge SG8 7RG
Tel: 01763 208008
Fax: 01763 208080
www.iconbooks.co.uk/wizard

Young Picador
(see Macmillan)

Zero to Ten
(see Evans Brothers)

DISTRIBUTORS

Ragged Bears
(Airlift Book Company)
8 The Arena
Mollison Avenue
Enfield
Middlesex EN3 7NL
Tel: 020 8804 0400
Fax: 020 8804 0044
www.ragged-bears.co.uk

Turnaround Publisher Service
Unit 3, Olympia Trading Estate
Coberg Road
Wood Green
London N22 6TZ
Tel: 020 8829 3000
Fax: 020 8881 5088
www.turnaround-psl-com

Academi

Mount Stuart House
Mount Stuart Square
Cardiff Bay
Cardiff CF10 5FQ
Contact: Peter Finch
Tel: 029 204 72266
post@academi.org www.academi.org

The Welsh National Literature
Promotion Agency has resources
available for poets and poetry.
They organise events and tours,
promote poets and poetry, offer
poetry advice, locate poetry publishers and provide financial help
to poets and to organisers wishing to book poets. The service is
only available to those in Wales.

Apples & Snakes
Performance Poetry

Battersea Arts Centre
Lavender Hill
London SW11 5TN
Tel: 020 7924 3410
info@applesandsnakes.org
www.applesandsnakes.org

Apples & Snakes is a performance
poetry organisation that has
has established a network for
performance poetry across the
UK. Education is at the core of its
mission and it carries out a wide
range of educational activities, of
which the extremely successful
Poets in Education Scheme is an
integral part. It providesresources
and advice for poets starting out
in performance poetry, general
information about the poetry
scene, and resources for teachers
including a selection of sample
lesson plans. Apples & Snakes
also develops community-based
performance poetry festivals,
tours and events, both in the
wider community and at its base
in Battersea Arts Centre.

The Arvon Foundation

42a Buckingham Palace Road
London SW1W 0RE
www.arvonfoundation.org

The Arvon Foundation is a
registered charity that runs residential creative writing courses at
centres in Devon, Shropshire,
Yorkshire and Inverness. The
courses are for people of all ages
and backgrounds and aim to
provide an inspirational space
and dedicated time to practise
the art of writing. They are
committed to making the
courses available to everyone,
regardless of their circumstances,
and fundraise to provide bursary
support for those requiring
financial assistance.

Centre for Literacy in Primary
Education (CLPE)

Webber Street
London, SE1 8QW
Tel: 020 7401 3382/3
Fax: 020 7928 4624
Email: info@clpe.co.uk
www.clpe.co.uk

CLPE is a resource centre, which
provides INSET courses for
primary teachers and others
concerned with language,
literacy, children's literature and
educational assessment. The
reference library contains a large
display of children's books,
including collections of picture
books, traditional stories and
poetry, and there is also a
teachers' reference library.
Poetry is a particular strength of
CLPE's library. The collection
encompasses nursery and action
rhymes, humorous poetry, general and thematic anthologies,
collections by individual poets,
song books and published collec-

tions of poetry by children. CLPE
currently hosts the children's
section of the South Bank Poetry
Library in a Poetry Zone alongside its own poetry collection.
CLPE publishes a variety of
different publications suitable for
teachers and parents, including
Hands on Poetry, A Year with Poetry
and *Look, No Hands!*, a cassette of
James Berry reading his own
poems. Publications also include
several anthologies of poetry by
Peckham school children, which
have resulted from local workshops.

The Children's Bookshow

Siân Williams
Tel: 020 8960 0602
Sianwilliams1@gmail.com

The Children's Bookshow was set
up in 2003 by Siân Williams and is
a national tour of children's writers and illustrators who perform
in theatres throughout England
during October and November of
each year. A programme of
school workshops runs alongside
the tour. Each tour has a theme;
these have included Folk and
Fairy Tales, Translation and
Poetry.

East-Side Educational Trust

Suite 16, Perseverance Works
37 Hackney Road
London E2 7NX
Tel: 020 7033 2380
Fax: 020 7613 3893
www.eastside.org.uk

East-Side Educational Trust is a
highly acclaimed and award-winning arts and educational charity
that introduces young people,
aged from 3-25, to literature and
the arts in London and assists in
raising their standards of achieve-

ment in language and literacy through the use of creative arts and drama. A new Resource Centre is being developed that will offer a wide variety of resources – such as special book collections on dance, drama, film, music, literature and visual arts, DVDs and CDs, masks and various equipment – that can be used in the planning of workshops, seminars and training and for the many different projects which take place in schools, colleges, professional venues and community settings. It will be open to creative practitioners, artists and facilitators active within arts education, and to young people and anyone with a specific interest in performing arts and education. The 'Universal Verse' poetry collection will be housed permanently in the Resource Centre.

Mini Mushaira

c/o 11 Donnington Road
Sheffield
South Yorkshire S2 2RF
Contact: Simon Fletcher &
Debjani Chatterjee
Tel: 01743 245004
simon@shrews1.fsnet.co.uk

Mini Mushaira are a group of multicultural poets and storytellers who seek to build cultural 'bridges' through their work with both children and adults. The four writers – Debjani Chatterjee and Brian G. D'Arcy in Sheffield, Simon Fletcher in Shrewsbury and Basir Sultan Kazmi in Manchester – give multilingual poetry performances and run poetry workshops throughout the country. They have also produced an anthology, *A Little Bridge*, published by Pennine Pens.

National Association of Writers in Education (NAWE)

PO Box 1
Sheriff Hutton
York YO60 7YU
Tel: 01653 618429
paul@nawe.co.uk
www.nawe.co.uk

NAWE is a national organisation that represents and supports writers, poets, teachers and all those involved in the development of creative writing in education. It publishes the magazine *Writing in Education* and holds a database of writers and poets who work in schools, colleges and the community and are available to search on the NAWE website.

Peterloo Poets

The Old Chapel
Sand Lane, Calstock
Cornwall PL18 9QX
Contact: Harry Chambers
www.peterloopoets.com

Peterloo Poets is a poetry publisher based in Cornwall that aims to publish quality work by new and neglected poets and to establish a Peterloo list of successive volumes of poets of proven worth. Although Peterloo is a publisher of adult poetry, they do run an annual poetry competition that has a 15-19 age group section with five prizes of £100 each. Poems must not exceed 40 lines and may be on any subject or theme and in any style or form, and must not have been previously published. A payment of £2.00 is required for each poem to a maximum of ten entries. For further details and an entry form visit the website.

The Poetry Archive

www.poetryarchive.org
www.poetryarchive.org/children's archive

The Poetry Archive is the world's premier online collection of recordings of poets reading their work. You can enjoy listening here, free of charge, to the voices of contemporary English-language poets and of poets from the past. Full recordings are available to purchase from the Poetry Book Society
www.poetrybookshoponline.com
The recordings are supported by resources for students and teachers as well as the general listener. The website also houses the Children's Poetry Archive, which is designed for 5 to11-year-olds and contains poems chosen specially for them, The Poetry Book Society and The Children's Poetry Bookshelf (see page 142).

The Poetry Can

Unit 11, 20-22 Hepburn Road
Bristol BS2 8UD
Contact: Colin Brown
Tel: 0117 943 6976
colin@poetrycan.demon.co.uk
www.poetrycan.com

The Poetry Can aim to encourage people within the Bristol and Bath areas to get involved in poetry activity. They run a programme of events and projects and support the creative and professional development of poets of all ages and levels of experience. Each year, high profile public events are held at both the Bath Literature Festival in March and the Bristol Poetry Festival in September. Poetry Can manage a number of projects that bring poetry into the community and develop new audiences for poetry, including projects in which poets work in schools. They also offer training with regular workshops as well as providing support and advice.

Poetry on Loan
Book Communications
Unit 116, The Custard Factory
Gibb Street
Birmingham B9 4AA
Contact: Jonathan Davidson
Tel: 0121 246 2770
jonathan@bookcommunications.co.uk
www.lit-net.org

Poetry on Loan is a joint promotion by public library authorities in the West Midlands who are working together to promote contemporary poetry by means of displays, poetry reading and writing groups and performances by top poets. Poetry on Loan takes place in 23 libraries across the region.

The Poetry Society
22 Betterton Street
London WC2H 9BU
Tel: 020 7420 9880
Fax: 020 7240 4818
Marketing@poetrysociety.org.uk
www.poetrysociety.org.uk

The Poetry Society exists to help poets and poetry thrive in Britain today. It is a membership organisation open to all and has around 4,000 members. The Society's magazine, *Poetry Review*, provides a forum for poems from both new and established poets and offers an overview of contemporary poetry. The *Poetry News* newsletter contains interviews with poets, information about events, competitions, festivals, magazines, advice and the poetry scene in general. The Poetry Society runs

a variety of projects to keep poetry flourishing in schools, libraries and the workplace. They also provide a specialist advice and information service 'Poetry Prescription' and Poetry Landmarks of Britain is often the first port of call on the website when researching poetry in a particular region. There is also a Poetry Café and The Poetry Studio is a venue for readings regularly hosted by the Poetry Society.

National Poetry Day takes place every year during the first week of October and aims to celebrate the art form of poetry and provide a platform for poets and poetry of all kinds. Each year a different theme is chosen and numerous events are held all around the country.

Poetry Translation Centre
London University
Room 404, School for Oriental and African Studies
Thornhaugh Street
London WC1H 0XG
Tel: 020 7898 4367
Fax: 020 7898 4239
ptc@soas.ac.uk
www.poetrytranslation.soas.ac.uk

The Poetry Translation Centre was set up to enrich poetry in English through making good translations of non-European poetry widely available and to give readers a deeper insight into the cultural history and background informing non-European poetry in a wide variety of languages.

The Seamus Heaney Centre for Poetry
46-48 University Road
Belfast BT7 1NN
Tel: 028 9097 1070
shc@qub.ac.uk
www.qub.ac.uk/heaneycentre

The Seamus Heaney Centre for Poetry is an international base for high-quality research and creative writing with a particular focus on poetry in modern Ireland. It houses an extensive library of contemporary poetry, hosts regular creative writing workshops, readings and lectures by visiting poets and scholars from around the world. It is also the custodian of the Seamus Heaney Media Archive.

Survivors' Poetry
Studio 11
Bickerton House
25-27 Bickerton Road
London N19 5JT
Tel: 02072 814 654
Fax: 02072 817 894
www.survivorspoetry.com

Survivors' Poetry is a national literature and performance charity. It is dedicated to celebrating the creative expression of survivors and to the promotion of poetry by survivors of mental distress. It comprises a network of 28 groups and more than 2,000 members worldwide. Survivors' Poetry provides workshops, performance readings, training courses and publications.

Northern Poetry Library

Morpeth Library
Gas House Lane
Morpeth
Northumberland NE61 1TA
Contact: Pat Hallam
Tel: 01670 534524
pathallam@northumberland.gov.uk

The Northern Poetry Library has the largest collection of contemporary poetry in England outside London. The collection includes 17,000 volumes of poetry as well as magazines covering English-language poetry, both adults' and children's, published since 1968. Membership is free to anyone living in the areas of Tyne and Wear, Durham, Northumberland, Cumbria and Cleveland. They have a searchable database and a postal lending service is available to members who pay return postage.

The Poetry Library

Level 5, Royal Festival Hall
London SE1 8XX
Tel: 020 7921 0943 / 0664
info@poetrylibrary.org.uk
www.poetrylibrary.org.uk

The Poetry Library aims to promote modern and contemporary British poetry. The Library collects all poetry in all formats published in English in this country (including translations from other languages), and a selection of publications from other countries. It is a free public library, housed at the South Bank Centre in London. Services include research support, loans of books and audio-visual items, group visits to the Library, loans to schools and other organisations, and a postal service to people with sight problems. The

core of the Library's children's section is formed by the Signal Collection of children's poetry books, which was donated to the Poetry Library in 1989. Since that date, the Library has collected nursery rhymes, traditional verse, verse novels and picture books with rhyming text, as well as collections and anthologies of poetry for children. Our enquiry service can help with all aspects of poetry for children.

The Scottish Poetry Library

5 Crichton's Close
Canongate
Edinburgh EH8 8DT
Tel: 0131 558 2876
Contact: Julie Johnstone
admin@spl.org.uk
www.spl.org.uk

The Scottish Poetry Library has a collection of contemporary poetry that includes written works, cassettes, CDs and videos. Poetry written in Scots, Gaelic and English is available, as well as historic Scottish poetry and contemporary works from around the world, magazines, a reading room for members, computerised references and searches and news cuttings. They also have collections for the visually impaired and outreach collections are held at other Scottish locations. All resources, advice and information are accessible, free of charge. There is a free borrowing service and a postal borrowing service at 50p per item, which includes freepost return label. Borrowing can also be done through the interlibrary loan system.

The Young Scottish Poetry Library is a dedicated children's section with a workshop programme and young people's and education website. Teachers can register for a free 'Poet in the Past' resource pack on *www.spl.org.uk/youngpeople*

Christopher Tower Poetry Prize

Tower Poetry
Christ Church
Oxford OX1 1DP
Tel/Fax: 01865 286591
info@towerpoetry.org.uk

The Christopher Tower Poetry Prize is an annual poetry competition that is open to 16-18-year-olds in UK schools and colleges. Poems must be no longer than 48 lines, on a different chosen theme each year. There are three prize categories – 1st (£3,000), 2nd (£1,000) and 3rd (£500). Each winner also receives a prize for their school.

The CLPE Poetry Award

(see address details above)

The CLPE Poetry Award was set up in 2003 to highlight an important branch of children's literature and ensure that it receives proper recognition. The award is presented annually for a book of poetry published in the preceding year. A pamphlet on the Award is published each year and is available for £2.50 (including postage and packing) and free to all CLPE subscribers.

The Corneliu M. Popescu Prize for European Poetry in Translation

(Administered by Poetry Society)

Named after Corneliu M. Popescu, translator of one of Romania's leading poets, Mihai Eminescu, this prize is awarded biennially to a collection of poetry which features poetry translated from a European language into English.

Foyle Young Poets of the Year Award

(Administered by Poetry Society)

This prestigious prize is open to anyone between the ages of 11 and 17 and consistently recognises and rewards some of the brightest future stars of the poetry world. The award is made possible by The Foyle Foundation, which distributes grants to charitable organisations in the areas of Learning, Arts and Health; it is administered by the Poetry Society. The winners of the 15-17 age range are given the opportunity to attend a week-long residential course at the prestigious Arvon Centre where they will be tutored by the judges of the competition. The winners in the 11-15 range receive a visit to their school from one of the Poetry Society's team of Poets in Schools. All winners are invited to attend a major awards ceremony in London on National Poetry Day and the winning poems will be published in a specially printed anthology. More information about the award may be found at *www.foyleyoungpoets.org*.

The Times Stephen Spender Prize for Poetry Translation

Administered by the Stephen Spender Memorial Trust
The Times Stephen Spender Prize
3 Old Wish Road
Eastbourne
East Sussex BN21 4JZ
www.stephen-spender.org

This annual competition was launched with the aim of encouraging schoolchildren and young people to try their hand at literary translation. Entrants are invited to translate a poem from any language, classical or modern, into English. There are cash prizes in three categories – Open, 18-and-Under and 14-and-Under – with all winning entries published in a booklet. For details and to read last year's winning entries, visit the website or email: *prize@times-spender.info* for a free copy of the booklet.

Poetry Matters

Tower Poetry
Christ Church
Oxford OX1 1DP
Tel/Fax: 01865 286591
info@towerpoetry.org.uk

Poetry Matters is an online poetry magazine that provides a fresh, dynamic perspective on poetry issues through a mix of news, reviews and comment. It will appeal to students in the final stages of secondary education, but its content and scope will also be of interest and relevance to the wider poetry community.

The Poetry Kit

50 Princesway
Wallasey
Merseyside CH45 4PR
Contact: Jim Bennett
info@poetrykit.org
www.poetrykit.org

Poetry Kit is a major poetry writers' resource site. Numerous listings including publishers, competitions, courses, funding, events, festivals and magazines. It also holds a Who's Who in Poetry and a listing of blogs and poets on the internet. Home of the internet-based 'Poetry Kit Magazine' and a monthly newsletter of competitions and events around the world.

The Poetry Zone

www.poetryzone.co.uk

The Poetry Zone is a website set up primarily to enable children and teenagers to publish their own poetry and reviews. Details of copyright and how to go about it are available on the 'How to Send Us your poems' part of the website. There is a great deal of useful information on the site from 'The Poetry Gallery' – a weekly round-up of the best poems that have been sent in; interviews with famous poets; a competition page; a 'Teacher Zone' full of ideas and resources including the Directory of Children's Poets plus the latest poetry releases; a 'Review' zone; 'Top Ten' poetry book selections for children, teenagers and adults; links to poetry sites; a feedback section and a 'What's On' – news about poetry events and the poetry shop with recommendations of poetry books.

A & C Black is publishing a *Poetry Writers' Yearbook 2007* edited by Gordon Kerr, price £12.99
ISBN: 0713675764

The *Poetry Writers' Yearbook* gives detailed listings of publishing companies, events and competitions. It provides information on funding, self-publishing and how you can survive and thrive as a poet. This new book includes a foreword by Andrew Motion and contributions from established poets George Szirtes, Colette Bryce and Carol Ann Duffy. Packed with useful contacts and advice, the *Poetry Writers' Yearbook* brings poets and audiences together and is an authoritative reference source.

Included here is a list of books that will be useful in the teaching of poetry.

Axed Between the Ears: A Poetry Anthology
Edited by David Kitchen
Heinemann (1987) PB £8.99
ISBN: 0 435 14530 4

Earshot: A Poetry Anthology
Edited by David Kitchen
Heinemann (1988) PB £8.99
ISBN: 0 435 14532 9

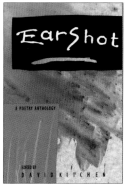

Both these collections are ideal as an introduction to poetry. *Axed Between the Ears* is for the 11-14 age range while *Earshot* is for the slightly older 14-16 group. Included are a selection of modern poets, whose poems are loosely grouped into themes so that two or more poems can be looked at together or one at a time. They include imaginative activities that involve discussion and creative writing and will win over the most reluctant readers of poetry.

Developing Poetry Skills: Reading Poetry 11-14
Geoff Barton
Heinemann (1998) PB £9.75
ISBN: 0 435 10412 8

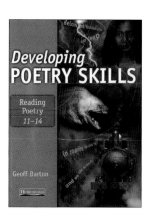

This ideal resource was written to meet the demands of reading poetry at KS3 and beyond and will provide students with the key skills necessary to develop an understanding of poetry as well as to make it fun and enjoyable. Divided into nine units with activities that develop through-out the book.

Discovering Poetry
Denise Scott
Heinemann (1993) PB £9.99
ISBN: 0 435 14042 6

Discovering Poetry contains over 100 accessible poems in a variety of genres and periods, plus lots of stimulating activities on the meaning, form and language of poetry suitable for KS3. A useful glossary provides explanations of poetic terms used throughout the book.

New Scottish Poetry
Gordon Liddell and Anne Gifford
Heinemann (2001) PB £9.50
ISBN: 0 435 15098 7

This collection of poetry will be of interest to any teachers who want to introduce Scottish poetry into their lessons. The anthology includes a host of Scottish poets together with translations and activities designed to help with writing, group discussion and individual presentation.

Our Thoughts are Bees: Writers Working with Schools
Mandy Coe and Jean Sprackland
Wordplay Press (2005) PB £10
ISBN: 0 9549634 0 7

This book gives advice on organ-ising exciting projects in schools, from the author's visit to the long-term residency. It examines the potential impact on young people's lives, and sets out a vision for the future of writing in education. Subjects include: how to book an author; working in museums and galleries; displays, performance and anthologies; funding; good practice; writers finding work in schools; residen-cies and day-visits; creative writ-ing in the classroom. It also has a foreword by Michael Morpurgo. The book is available from *www.wordplaypress.com*

Poetry Then and Now: Approaches to Pre-Twentieth Century Poetry
Sheila Hales
Heinemann (1994) PB £9.75
ISBN: 0 435 14043 4

This anthology is ideal for KS3 and is organised thematically with contemporary and classic

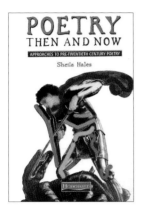

POETRY
THEN AND NOW
APPROACHES TO PRE-TWENTIETH CENTURY POETRY
Sheila Hales

poetry placed alongside each other to stimulate discussion. Oral work is particularly encouraged with a host of stimulating, well-structured activities including drama, games, and performances that will help bring the poems alive in the classroom. A glossary of technical terms is also included.

Selected Poetry (Caribbean Writers Series)
Derek Walcott (1993) PB £7.40
ISBN: 0 435 91197

This is a selection of Nobel prize-winning poet Derek Walcott, who was born and brought up on the Caribbean Island of St Lucia. It is an excellent introduction to his poetry for the 14+ age group, spanning over 20 years and covering a whole range of different themes from the nature of memory and creative imagination to history and politics, the landscape of the West Indies and love and marriage.

Interactive Poetry 11-14 CD-ROM and Teacher's Guide Pack
Heinemann (2006) £250 (+VAT)
Interactive Poetry 11-14 Student Book £9.00

Interactive Poetry 11-14 Evaluation Pack (contains the CD-ROM Pack and free copy of the Student Book) £250 (+VAT)

The content of this interactive poetry CD includes work by Norman Silver, John Agard and Elizabeth Jennings. Themes include Playing with Words; Poem Pairing; and Poetic Devices. There are three poems for each poet and every poem features two activities, two images, and an audio reading; one of each set of three poems has a video clip.

A Year with Poetry: Teachers Write About Teaching Poetry
Edited by Myra Barrs and Michael Rosen
CLPE PB £11.00 (£9.00 for CLPE School Network)
ISBN: 1 872267 12 2

A Year with Poetry is the story of a group of ten London teachers as they record their journey into teaching poetry and the writing of poetry. Guided by Michael Rosen during their year-long workshop, the group met several times to read, write and talk about poetry and to share poetry from classrooms. At the end of the year the teachers wrote about their experiences for other teachers to read. Each chapter records not only what their children achieved with them, but also their own personal development. Illustrated throughout with black-and-white photographs and children's work from the schools involved, this book encourages teachers to come together and share their work in poetry.

Hands on Poetry: Using Poetry in the Classroom
Myra Barrs and Sue Ellis
CLPE PB £9.00 (£7.00 for CLPE Schools Network)
ISBN: 872267 07 6

Hands on Poetry helps teachers to put poetry within the reach of all children. It contains a broad range of ideas and activities including suggestions for developing children's understanding of poetry through different art forms such as music, drama and art as well as reading and writing. This highly illustrated publication will provide an invaluable resource for primary teachers. It contains suggestions for ways in which you can involve children in the pleasures of listening to poems, reading them aloud – alone or with others – and writing their own.

Look No Hands
A taped collection of poetry for children by James Berry
Readings by James Berry and Jan Blake, music by Keith Waithe
CLPE Audio cassette £7.75 (£5.75 for CLPE Schools Network)

This audio cassette contains an exciting collection of James Berry's poems and rhymes for children, which have been specially selected for the classroom. They range from lyrical pictures of Caribbean childhood to songs, modern rap-inspired poems and poems with humorous themes. The poems will benefit from being replayed and studied in classrooms but are also immediately accessible to young listeners.

DETAILS OF ALL CLPC PUBLICATIONS ARE AVAILABLE FROM THEIR WEBSITE: *www.clpe.co.uk*

If you enjoyed Michael Rosen's Foreword and love his poems here are two books that you might enjoy. They aren't poetry but they're great reads.

You're thinking about doughnuts
Michael Rosen
ISBN 1 903015 03 0 £4.99

Frank's mum cleans the local museum on a Friday night and usually Frank goes to spend the evening with his Gran: that is until Gran is ill and Frank has to go to the museum with his Mum. Left on his own in the deserted museum with all the exhibits, Frank feels nervous and when a skeleton comes alive and insists that he is "Thinking About Doughnuts", terror takes over. However the skeleton turns out to be harmless and is keen to introduce Frank to all the other inhabitants of the museum and Frank enjoys a unique history and geography lesson.

An informative and hilarious read.

You're thinking about tomatoes
Michael Rosen
ISBN 1 903015 44 8 £4.99

It's happening to Frank again. This time he's on a school trip to a stately home when a black girl walks out of her picture and insists that Frank helps her find her real name and real identity. And before he knows it Frank is on another merry-go-round through time and space and learning all about how things get to what they are and where they are. As well as Not-Sheba the slave girl, there is a celebrity crazy Mummy to speed Frank on his adventures.

Another learn while you laugh book.

If you enjoy rhymes you might enjoy the wonderful full-colour, comic style books about Stanley Bagshaw.

Our Stanley is a good natured idiot, who always manages to come out on top. They're all written in rhyming couplets, which makes them even more fun to read! All the books start in the same way, just to give you a taster.

> *In Huddersgate, famed for its tramlines,*
> *Up North where it's boring and slow.*
> *Stanley Bagshaw resides with his grandma,*
> *At number 4 Prince Albert Row.*

Stanley Bagshaw and the short-sighted football trainer Bob Wilson
£4.99 ISBN 1 903015 26 X £4.99

When the home team Huddersgate is playing at home, Stanley is desperate to see the game but can't get a ticket. Wandering around the dressing rooms looking for autographs, Stanley finds himself in goal and saving the match!

Stanley Bagshaw and the Mafeking Square Cheese Robbery Bob Wilson
£4.99 ISBN 1 903015 31 6

This time, entirely by accident, Stanley manages to foil dangerous robbers in Mafeking Square, Huddersgate.

Stanley Bagshaw and the fourteen-foot wheel
Bob Wilson £4.99 ISBN 1 903015 40 5

Our Stanley agrees to watch a machine at a factory but falls asleep. The result is a fourteen-foot wheel that makes its way through Huddersgate causing hilarious levels of chaos.

Stanley Bagshaw and the twenty-two ton whale
Bob Wilson £4.99 ISBN 1 903015 50 2

When a twenty-two ton whale is trapped in the canal, no one knows what to do until Stanley Bagshaw finds a way to get the whale to turn round and swim back to the sea. Of course an awful lot of people get very wet.